W9-CJL-283

The Collector's Bach

THE
COLLECTOR'S
BACH

by Nathan Broder

GREENWOOD PRESS, PUBLISHERS
WESTPORT, CONNECTICUT

Library of Congress Cataloging in Publication Data

Broder, Nathan.
  The collector's Bach.

  Reprint of the 1958 ed. published by Lippincott,
Philadelphia, which was issued as no. K3 of Keystone
books in music.
    1. Bach, Johann Sebastian, 1685-1750--Discography.
2. Bach, Johann Sebastian, 1685-1750. Works. I. Title.
II. Series: Keystone books in music ; K3.
[ML156.5.B2B7 1978]   016.7899'12   77-28265
ISBN 0-313-20240-0

This is a considerably revised version of a discography that was written at the suggestion of Mr. Roland Gelatt, music editor of *High Fidelity* magazine, and that appeared in three instalments in that periodical. I am grateful to Mr. Charles Fowler, publisher of *High Fidelity,* for permission to use the material here.

N. B.

This edition published by arrangement with J. B. Lippincott Company, Philadelphia, New York.

Reprinted in 1978 by Greenwood Press, Inc.
51 Riverside Avenue, Westport, CT. 06880

Printed in the United States of America

10 9 8 7 6 5 4 3 2 1

TO MITCHELL LAUB

Contents

JOHANN SEBASTIAN BACH

Biographical Sketch

Born Eisenach, March 21, 1685; died
Leipzig, July 28, 1750

BACH'S BIRTHPLACE is in Thuringia, a district in
western Saxony. Except for a short period in his
youth and one or two trips later on, he never left
south-central Germany. He was a musician by trade,
coming from a family that had produced musicians
in a steady stream ever since the sixteenth century.
In seventeenth-century Germany it was expected
that a man would embrace his father's profession,
but what is remarkable in Bach's case is the way in
which the profession seized upon the man. Bach
was an avid student of his art from his early child-
hood to the end of his days.

His father taught him to play the violin and viola.
When both of his parents died, Sebastian, now
about ten, went to live with an older brother,
Johann Christoph, organist at Ohrdruf, a town some
thirty miles away. From him Sebastian learned to
play the clavier (a term applied to any stringed
keyboard instrument) and organ. From him, too,
Sebastian probably had his first lessons in composition. The school in Ohrdruf was an unusually
progressive one for the time; Sebastian, who was an
excellent student, received a solid grounding in Latin

and other subjects, especially religion. It was probably this school's emphasis on theological subjects that helped to instill or develop in Bach the faith that remained firmly and profoundly his for the rest of his life.

In 1700, at the age of fifteen, he journeyed two hundred miles north to Lüneburg. There he was enrolled as a soprano in the choir. He lived in the buildings connected with St. Michael's Church, and received a monthly stipend and a share of the fees paid to the choir for special performances, as at weddings and funerals. Here Bach found a remarkably well-stocked library of seventeenth-century vocal music by German and Italian composers, including such masters as Monteverdi and Schütz among the older men and Buxtehude among contemporaries. Bach had already shown, at his brother's house in Ohrdruf, an eager curiosity about any music he could lay his hands on. One can imagine the excitement with which he must have approached the treasures in the Lüneburg library.

When his voice changed, he was kept on as an accompanist. He studied the music of Georg Böhm, organist at St. John's Church in Lüneburg, and took at least one walking trip to Hamburg, thirty miles away, to hear the celebrated Reinken play the organ there. He is also said to have trudged the sixty miles to Celle, where the Duke of Lüneburg-Celle maintained a lively musical establishment and favored French music.

In 1703 Bach was back in Thuringia. At the age of eighteen he was already so highly regarded as an organist that he had been asked by the authorities at Arnstadt to test a new organ that had just been installed in St. Boniface's Church there. After he had played on it and given his opinion, he was hired as organist. As part of his job he had to train boys for the chorus, a task that could not have been easy, because it would seem from a contemporary report that the choristers were what we would call juvenile delinquents. Two years after he was established at Arnstadt, Bach applied for a leave of absence and traveled three hundred miles to visit Buxtehude at Lübeck. Although his leave was for one month, he was so fascinated by the programs directed by Buxtehude that he stayed away four months. A few weeks after he returned he was summoned before the consistory and admonished, not only for overstaying his leave but also for confusing the congregation by "making many surprising variations in the chorale" when accompanying the hymns.

Unhappy at Arnstadt, Bach moved in 1707 to Mühlhausen, as organist at St. Blaise's Church. Soon afterwards he married his cousin, Maria Barbara Bach, daughter of an organist. It was here that Bach wrote *Gott ist mein König* (Cantata No. 71), the only one of his cantatas that was published during his lifetime. After only one year at Mühlhausen, he accepted a more lucrative appointment at near-by Weimar.

Weimar was the seat of Wilhelm Ernst, Duke of Sachsen-Weimar, a sober, cultured, pious, and conscientious ruler. He was fond of music, but, like his new employee and unlike other princes of the time, he did not particularly care for the stage. He required the court orchestra, including its newest member, to wear the uniform of the Hungarian hussars. Bach's duties were to play the violin in the orchestra, to lead the Duke's chamber musicians, to serve as court organist, and to compose and conduct cantatas and other works. His house was full of pupils and, in the course of time, his own children. It was a busy life, and yet, despite all distractions, he produced a steady stream of cantatas and organ and clavier works. In 1717 there was an incident that received a good deal of publicity throughout Germany. A French organist by the name of Louis Marchand, considered one of the most skillful performers of his time, happened to be in Dresden when Bach was visiting there. Bach challenged him to a sight-reading contest. Marchand accepted, and a meeting was arranged at the house of a local nobleman. When the appointed time came, however, it was learned that Marchand had left town that morning, thus tacitly acknowledging defeat; and Bach played alone for the pleased and admiring crowd.

By this time Bach was preparing to leave Weimar. For various reasons—among them a considerably higher salary, and disappointment because he had not received a promotion he felt he deserved—he accepted, in 1717, an appointment as Kapellmeister to Prince Leopold of Anhalt-Cöthen. He could not take up his new duties, however, until he received a formal release from Duke Wilhelm Ernst. This the Duke at first refused to give him, and when Bach boldly insisted, he was clapped into jail. After a month in prison, during which some writers think he planned the *Orgelbüchlein*, the Duke reluctantly let him go.

Prince Leopold was a good musician; he could

sing, and could play well the violin, the viola da gamba, and the clavier. When Bach arrived at Cöthen in December, 1717, he took charge of the Prince's musical establishment. The orchestra, known as the Collegium Musicum, comprised eighteen players, augmented by additional performers on special occasions. In Cöthen Bach was not required to play the organ or to compose music for religious services. Consequently his output in these years is mostly secular and instrumental—much clavier music, including the English and French Suites and Part I of the *Well-Tempered Clavier*; the works for violin solo and 'cello solo and much chamber music; the three violin concertos, the six "Brandenburg" Concertos, and at least two of the four orchestral suites. In July, 1720, Maria Barbara, his wife of thirteen years, died. She had been a loving helpmeet, and had borne him six children. The two oldest surviving sons, Wilhelm Friedemann (born 1710) and Carl Philipp Emanuel (born 1714), together with a still-unborn half-brother, were to extend the musical fame of the Bach name. In December, 1721, Bach took as his second wife the twenty-year-old singer Anna Magdalena Wilcken. A week later, Prince Leopold, too, married. It soon became apparent that his bride did not share her husband's taste in music or his regard for his favorite musician. Bach's position became awkward, and he began to look about for another post. A position being vacant at Leipzig, he applied for it. There were several other candidates, and Bach was by no means the one with the strongest support. Invited to write a Passion as a kind of test piece, he produced the *St. John Passion* at Leipzig in March,

1723. In April the candidate favored by the City Council withdrew for reasons of his own, and Bach was appointed.

Bach's duties in Leipzig were manifold and rather complicated. As Cantor of St. Thomas's School, he superintended the musical instruction of the pupils and did some teaching himself. He was also in general charge of the music in four of the city's churches, though he personally led the performances in only two of them—St. Thomas's and St. Nicholas's. He was expected to compose, or provide, a cantata for most Sundays as well as for special festivals, and a Passion each year. He was also sometimes called upon to write music for funerals of prominent citizens (most of the motets were written for this purpose) and for weddings of prosperous couples. Bach also had a tenuous official connection with the music at St. Paul's, the University chapel; the confused state of this relationship gave rise to much bickering between the composer and the University authorities. In 1729 he became conductor of one of the University's extracurricular organizations, a Collegium Musicum. All this obviously constituted a heavy schedule, and Bach gradually delegated more and more work to subordinates so that he could devote as much time as possible to composing. On Good Friday of 1729 he produced the *St. Matthew Passion*. In 1731 he published the first part of the *Clavier-Uebung*, consisting of the six Partitas for clavier. In 1733, anxious to secure the title of court composer to the Elector of Saxony, he offered that ruler a Lutheran Mass, consisting of a Kyrie and Gloria. The Elector was busy with other matters, and these two movements of the B minor Mass went unnoticed. The appointment came three years later. During the Leipzig years Bach apparently took up some of his early organ works and revised them. In the 1740's he published the *Goldberg Variations,* Part II of the *Well-Tempered Clavier,* and the *Musical Offering.* The last-named work was the result of a visit in 1747 to his son, Carl Philipp Emanuel, then employed at the court of Frederick the Great in Potsdam. The music-loving Frederick was astonished at Bach's improvisations on a theme provided by the King. When Bach returned home, he developed Frederick's theme into a set of fugues and canons and sent it to the King as a "Musical Offering." Toward the end of his life his eyesight began to fail. An operation was unsuccessful, and Bach's final compositions were dictated to his son-in-law. He passed away at a quarter to nine on Tuesday evening, July 28, 1750, at the age of sixty-five, leaving his second wife and nine children surviving from a total of nineteen.

We know very little of Bach's inner life apart from his music. His general outward appearance has been established by some well-made portraits. From the meager correspondence that remains we know that he was an indomitable fighter, insisting on his rights with bulldog tenacity whenever he thought they were being infringed. Though never wealthy, he always earned enough to keep his family fairly comfortable. He apparently moved with ease in the professional circles of Weimar, Cöthen, and Leipzig, and numbered among his friends educators, cultured laymen, and high officials of the clergy. The eyewitness accounts tell mostly of his astounding skill as an organist and of his extraordinary improvisations. Throughout his life he was called upon to examine and test new organs, to recommend improvements in old ones, so profound was his knowledge of the instrument. His even more profound knowledge of the craft of composition was not so widely recognized.

Except to the audience on the occasion for which they were written, most of his grandest works could not be known, because they remained unpublished for many years after his death. Moreover, when Bach died his music was already regarded as old-fashioned. For during the last two or three decades of his life there had begun a change in style with such revolutionary consequences that the music of his youngest son, Johann Christian (born 1735), belongs to an entirely different era. Yet it is not true, as is sometimes stated, that Bach's music was completely ignored in the generations immediately following him. The little that was known was highly regarded in small enclaves here and there. Vienna contained one such corner; there Mozart transcribed some of the fugues, and Beethoven gave his pupils the *Well-Tempered Clavier* to study. But it was not until Mendelssohn's celebrated revival of the *St. Matthew Passion* at Berlin in 1829 that the musical world in general began to wonder what other Bachian treasures lay hidden. More and more works were uncovered, and in 1850 the Bach Gesellschaft was organized for the purpose of publishing the master's complete works. Fifty years later the final, forty-sixth, volume appeared.

THE WORKS ARE listed here in the order in which they appear in Wolfgang Schmieder's thematic catalogue, the *Bach-Werke-Verzeichnis* (Leipzig, 1950). This is not a chronological catalogue, like the Köchel of Mozart or the Deutsch of Schubert. Instead the works are first divided into categories and then numbered continuously from 1 to 1080, beginning with the sacred cantatas. The Schmieder has unfortunately come to be abbreviated "BWV," but we use the more sensible (and internationally understandable) "S."

No attempt is made here to go into the vexed question of the interpretation of Bach's ornaments or to enter the controversy of harpsichord versus organ as the continuo keyboard instrument in the religious choral works.

The cases where modern instruments are used instead of those specified by Bach, *i.e.*, flute instead of recorder, are noted.

The quality of the recording may be assumed to be adequate or better unless the contrary is stated. Any remarks about surface noises refer to the writer's disks and are not necessarily true of other copies of the same issue. Such remarks are included here merely as warnings to the prospective purchaser.

No account is taken here of individual songs

and chorale harmonizations; of transcriptions of organ works for other media, such as orchestra or piano; or of individual movements from larger works and the numerous transcriptions of some of those movements.

In the case of vocal works, the record companies supply the original texts and English translations, unless otherwise indicated.

The order of the listing at the end of each item is intended to reflect the order of merit in the opinion of the reviewer.

Listings in brackets indicate recordings that were not available to the writer.

All records are single twelve-inch disks, unless otherwise indicated.

The second and subsequent citations of the same item are listed in abbreviated form.

A number of items listed are no longer in the catalogues, but they are retained here because they may still be available in some shops.

VOCAL WORKS

THERE IS surely nothing more that needs to be said about the *St. Matthew Passion* and the B minor Mass, two of the towering creations of the human mind. The gigantic fresco of the Passion presents a drama of sorrow and compassion that has never been surpassed in music. As for the Mass, I expect when I awake on Judgment Day to hear angelic choirs filling the heavens with the rolling triplets of the Sanctus. Since both of these works are available in good recordings, there is no reason why everyone should not be, or become, familiar with them.

No one can truly understand Bach's achievement, however, who has not penetrated into the world of the sacred cantatas. It is well known that Bach was a profoundly religious man, but just how deeply religious he was can be best understood when we see how the varying texts of these cantatas, insipid though some of them may seem to us, set his creative imagination on fire. Naturally, not all of these numerous works are on the same high level. The astonishing thing is how many of them are filled with a burning intensity.

It has frequently been pointed out that this important portion of Bach's output is closed off to us because complete cantatas are so seldom performed. In one way, this is no longer true. More than a fourth of the cantatas are now available on LP recordings. But in another way it is still true, at least to a certain extent. The mere fact that a cantata has been recorded does not necessarily mean that Bach has been truly, or even fairly, represented. The proper performance of Bach requires a combination of sensitiveness, imagination, and historical knowledge that is unfortunately all too rare. Many conductors and singers seem to freeze into a knot when confronted with a Bach score, as though they were convinced that any composer who did not sprinkle his pages liberally with expression marks must have had ice in his veins. It is true, of course, that Bach's music does not call for the kind of treatment that, say, Chopin's does. But it is equally true that the mechanical rigidity with which it is often performed misrepresents it fatally.

From this point of view, then, the recordings of Bach's vocal works may be said to fall into three groups: those in which the performers' insight, knowledge, and skill do something like justice to the music; those in which enough of these qualities are present to render the performances acceptable for want of better ones; and those that are mere note-reading and consequently worse than nothing. It will be seen that the second group is the most numerous, the first least so.

THE CANTATAS

No. 1, WIE SCHOEN LEUCHTET DER MORGENSTERN

Composed at Leipzig in the 1730s or '40s for Annunciation Day. This work, in keeping with the occasion for which it was written, breathes joy and good cheer from almost every measure of the lovely first chorus, the delightful soprano aria, and the lighthearted tenor aria. Miss Weber is not quite up to the cruelly long phrases of her aria and has to break them up to catch a breath. Mr. Krebs manages his very difficult aria acceptably. The chorus, like many others, is weak in the tenor department and sounds as though it should have been closer to the microphone.

——Gunthild Weber (s); Helmut Krebs (t); Hermann Schey (bs); Berlin Motet Choir; Berlin Philharmonic Orchestra, Fritz Lehmann, cond. ARCHIVE ARC 3063 (with Cantata No. 4).

No. 4, CHRIST LAG IN TODESBANDEN

Composed at Mühlhausen or Weimar, probably between 1708 and 1714, for Easter Day. This powerful and moving work, dominated by the idea of death rather than that of the Resurrection, has an unusual structure. Each of the seven verses of Luther's hymn is set as a separate movement and the whole is prefaced by a brief but very expressive *sinfonia*. There are no recitatives, no Italian-style *da capo* arias.

To make a choice among the three recordings is difficult. For beauty of choral tone and firmness of line, the palm—it seems to me—belongs to Shaw. His version employs an organ for the continuo in some movements but a harpsichord in Verses 4 and 6. In Verse 5 he uses a trumpet (not indicated in the score) to reinforce the chorale tune in the violins. Prohaska uses an organ throughout; his interpretation of the *sinfonia* is more dramatic than the other two; and he is favored with the quietest surfaces. In Verse 4 he has an unindicated trombone strengthening the *cantus firmus* in the altos. Lehmann's chorus is perhaps second best as regards tone and clarity. An organ is employed for the continuo, and he takes fewer liberties—that is, he sticks to the disposition of performing forces called for in the score. In Verse 3 he uses a solo tenor instead of the several tenors employed by Shaw and Prohaska, and one bass instead of several in Verse 5. The latter part is excellently sung by Fischer-Dieskau, who, however, avoids the great plunge down to E-sharp below the staff on the word "death" and alights too comfortably on the tone an octave higher.

——Robert Shaw Chorale and Orchestra, Robert Shaw, cond. RCA Victor lm 9035 (with Motet No. 3, *Jesus, Dearest Master*).

——Choir and Orchestra of the Bach Guild, Felix Prohaska, cond. Bach Guild bg 511 (with Cantata No. 140).

——Helmut Krebs (t); Dietrich Fischer-Dieskau (bs); Chorus of the State School for Music, Frankfurt; Göttingen Bach Festival Orchestra, Fritz Lehmann, cond. Archive arc 3063 (with Cantata No. 1).

No. 6. Bleib' bei uns

Leipzig, probably 1736, for Easter Monday. The magnificent opening chorus, with its deeply moving part-writing and poignant harmonies and the rich, reedy sound of the oboes, is enough to place this cantata among the great masterworks. The alto aria, which follows, is on the same high plane. It is nicely sung here, with a warm tone and good phrasing. The rest of the work is not quite up to the exalted standard set by Bach in the first two movements. Rather boomy bass in No. 1, but elsewhere the recording is realistic, the disembodied tone of the sopranos in No. 3 being especially well caught.

——Hetty Plümacher (a); Werner Hohmann (t); Bruno Müller (bs); Stuttgart Choral Society and Bach Orchestra, Hans Grischkat, cond. RENAISSANCE x 34 (with Cantata No. 19).

No. 9, Es ist das Heil

Leipzig, probably 1731, for the Sixth Sunday after Trinity. Another fine opening chorus, in which reverently joyful figures curl about the chorale. Outstanding too is the expressive melody of the wide-ranging tenor aria (No. 3). The arias are competently sung, but the recitatives, for bass, are inflexible and mechanical. Performance in general acceptable.

——Claire Fassbender-Luz (s); Eva Drager (a); Claus Stemann (t); Bruno Müller (bs); Stuttgart Choral Society; Stuttgart Bach Orchestra, Hans Grischkat, cond. RENAISSANCE x 37 (with Cantata No. 137).

No. 11, LOBET GOTT IN SEINEN REICHEN

Leipzig, between 1730 and 1740, for Ascension. This splendid work was called by Bach an oratorio, but in mood and structure it is much like other cantatas. While the Lyrichord version is no shining model of Bach performance and the recording has considerable surface noise, it is much to be preferred to the London version on many counts. Its soloists, except for the alto, are better; its chorus is stronger and clearer; and its balances are more just. In the London recording the sound of the chorus is frequently weak and blurred, the important woodwind parts are sometimes inaudible, and the lovely soprano aria in Part II is ruthlessly cut. The only redeeming feature of that disk is Ferrier's warm and appealing singing of the great alto aria in Part I, later used by Bach in the Agnus Dei of the B minor Mass. The Lyrichord uses an organ for the continuo, is sung in German, and supplies texts in German and English. The London employs a harpsichord, is done in English, and provides no text.

——Claire Fassbender-Luz (s); Ruth Michaelis (a); Werner Hohmann (t); Bruno Müller (bs); Swabian Choral Singers; Stuttgart Bach Orchestra, Hans Grischkat, cond. LYRICHORD LL 34.

——Eva Mitchell (s); Kathleen Ferrier (a); William Herbert (t); William Parsons (bs); Cantata Singers; Jacques Orchestra, Reginald Jacques, cond. LONDON LL 845 (with Cantata No. 67 and *Jesu, Joy of Man's Desiring* from Cantata No. 147).

No. 19, ES ERHUB SICH EIN STREIT

Leipzig, 1725 or 1726, for St. Michael's Day. The mighty opening chorus depicts the struggle between

St. Michael and his angels and Satan and his hosts. In the Grischkat version it becomes a rather cheerful piece; in the Lehmann, it is slower, four-square, and rigidly metrical. In neither is there any trace of the grandeur of this musical fresco. For the rest, there is not much to choose between the two recordings. Renaissance has more surface noise and a better soprano. Decca's recitatives are less metronomic and its tenor has a more attractive voice, but he does little to mitigate the excessive length of his aria. There is no visible separation between movements on either disk.

——Agnes Giebel (s); Claus Stemann (t); Bruno Müller (bs); Stuttgart Choral Society; Tonstudio Orchestra, Hans Grischkat, cond. RENAISSANCE X 34 (with Cantata No. 6).

——Gunthild Weber (s); Helmut Krebs (t); Hermann Schey (bs); Berlin Motet Choir; Berlin Philharmonic Orchestra, Fritz Lehmann, cond. ARCHIVE ARC 3065 (with Cantata No. 79).

No. 21, ICH HATTE VIEL BERKUEMMERNIS

Mühlhausen and Weimar, 1714 and earlier, "for any season." That this early work is one of the relatively popular cantatas is understandable, for it is full of a youthful fervor and has a wide range of expressiveness, from the tortured dissonances of the soprano aria in Part I to the triumphant joy of the final chorus. On the whole, both performances are acceptable. Both solo tenors are good and both basses little more than adequate. Of the two sopranos Schwaiger's voice is the cooler, with scarcely any vibrancy or intensity; but since the part was probably written for a boy, the color of her voice is perhaps closer to what Bach had in mind. Lehmann's chorus is better balanced in itself and in relation to the orchestra, and his performance of the wonderful chorus *Sei wieder zufrieden* and the great final movement has more intensity than Sternberg's.

——Rosl Schwaiger (s); Hugues Cuenod (t); Alois Pernerstorfer (bs); Vienna Symphony Orchestra; Vienna Chamber Choir, Jonathan Sternberg, cond. BACH GUILD BG 501.

——Gunthild Weber (s); Helmut Krebs (t); Hermann Schey (bs); Berlin Motet Choir; Berlin Philharmonic Orchestra, Fritz Lehmann, cond. ARCHIVE ARC 3064.

No. 31, DER HIMMEL LACHT, DIE ERDE JUBILIERET

For Easter Sunday; composed at Weimar in 1715 but later revised. The festive opening "sonata" (with trumpets and drums) and the first chorus express the joy of Easter Day. Thereafter the librettist's thoughts turn toward death. The fine tenor aria (No. 6) is somewhat operatic in feeling. The crown of the work, it seems to me, is the exquisitely tender and lovely soprano aria (No. 8) with obbligato oboe, in the course of which the violins and violas gently introduce, with moving effect, the first verses of a chorale. This chorale is then taken up by the entire chorus and orchestra for the conclusion (No. 9). The soprano and the unnamed oboist are particularly good in No. 8. Otherwise the performance is acceptable, although the tenors of the chorus are too faint.

——Anny Felbermayer (s); Waldemar Kmentt (t); Walter Berry (bs); Vienna Chamber Orchestra and Akademie Choir, Felix Prohaska, cond. BACH GUILD BG 512 (with Seven Easter Chorales).

No. 32, LIEBSTER JESU, MEIN VERLANGEN

Leipzig, probably late 1730s, for the First Sunday after Epiphany. This is a "dialogus" for soprano and bass, with the chorus entering only for the final chorale. The first movement is a wonderful aria for soprano with obbligato oboe, expressing ineffable longing for Jesus. In No. 4, a conversation between the soloists, the soprano has some ecstatic arioso passages. The singers join in No. 5, rejoicing gaily in a dancelike rhythm. Scherchen's version is the more imaginative and moving. Both of the basses are good enough, but Scherchen's soprano is superior to Reinhardt's.

——Magda Laszlo (s); Alfred Poell (bs); Vienna Akademiechor; Orchestra of the Vienna State Opera, Hermann Scherchen, cond. WESTMINSTER XWN 18391 (with Cantata No. 152).

——Agnes Giebel (s); Bruno Müller (bs); Pro Musica Chorus and Orchestra (Stuttgart), Rolf Reinhardt, cond. Vox PL 7340 (with Cantata No. 57).

No. 34, O EWIGES FEUER

For Whitsuntide; an arrangement, made about 1740, of an earlier wedding cantata. There are two fine big choruses, a couple of brief *secco* recitatives, and a calmly sweet alto aria. The "eternal flame" burns very low in this performance. The chorus is no better than mediocre, and the alto has a tremolo.

——Lorna Sydney (a); Hugues Cuenod (t); Alois Pernerstorfer (bs); Vienna Chamber Choir and

Symphony Orchestra, Jonathan Sternberg, cond.
BACH GUILD BG 502 (with Cantata No. 56).

No. 39, BRICH DEM HUNGRIGEN DEIN BROT

Leipzig, probably 1732, for the First Sunday after
Trinity. The big and very expressive opening chorus,
with its curiously descriptive accompaniment, is the
outstanding movement in this work, along with a
fine accompanied recitative for alto. Miss Weber
again has trouble with phrasing—her breathing is
frequent and audible—but otherwise she is adequate, as are the other performers.
——Gunthild Weber (s); Lore Fischer (a); Hermann Schey (bs); Berlin Motet Choir; Berlin Philharmonic Orchestra, Fritz Lehmann, cond. ARCHIVE
ARC 3066 (with Cantata No. 105).

No. 41, JESU, NUN SEI GEPREISET

Leipzig, 1736 or about 1740, for New Year's Day.
Lighthearted joy is the predominating mood of the
opening chorus. This is followed by a lovely, pas-
torale-like aria for soprano, a tenor aria with obbligato violoncello piccolo, and a final chorale which
is especially interesting because of the interpolations of part of the instrumental ritornel from the
first chorus. The continuo part is performed on a
piano, and the obbligato in the tenor aria is played,
very beautifully, on an ordinary cello. The chorus
is slightly blurred at first, but soon becomes clearer.
The tone of both chorus and orchestra is unusually
good, and for once one can hear the tenors clearly.
In the reviewer's set this side is wrongly labeled, the
label being the same as on the other side (which
contains arias).

——Eileen Farrell (s); Carol Smith (a); Jan Peerce (t); Norman Farrow (bs); Robert Shaw Chorale and Orchestra, Robert Shaw, cond. Two 12-in. RCA Victor lm 6023 (with Cantatas Nos. 42 and 60, and arias and duets from other cantatas).

No. 42, Am Abend aber desselbigen Sabbats

Leipzig, 1731, for the First Sunday after Easter. This is one of the great masterworks. Among its peaks are the meltingly beautiful *sinfonia,* which would make a wonderful piece for an orchestral program; the gorgeously rich alto aria (No. 3); and the triumphant bass aria (No. 6). The soloists sing acceptably and the orchestra is very fine. A piano is used for the continuo.

——Eileen Farrell (s); Carol Smith (a); Jan Peerce (t); Norman Farrow (bs); Robert Shaw Chorale and Orchestra, Robert Shaw, cond. Two 12-in. RCA Victor lm 6023 (with Cantatas Nos. 41 and 60, and arias and duets from other cantatas).

No. 46, Schauet doch und sehet

Leipzig, middle 1720s, for the Tenth Sunday after Trinity. A powerful work. The first chorus, tragic and full of poignant dissonance, was later used in the *Qui tollis* of the B minor Mass. In the dramatic bass aria (No. 3) thunder rumbles in the basses and lightning flashes in the trumpet. Unfortunately, only Cuenod does justice to his part (the accompanied recitative for tenor, No. 2); the other soloists and the chorus are not quite up to this magnificent music.

——Lorna Sydney (a); Hugues Cuenod (t); Alois Pernerstorfer (bs); Vienna Symphony Orchestra

and Chamber Choir, Jonathan Sternberg, cond.
BACH GUILD BG 503 (with Cantata No. 104).

No. 50, NUN IST DAS HEIL UND DIE KRAFT

A single movement, of imposing strength, for double
chorus and orchestra and believed to have once
formed a part of a cantata. Well performed here.
—Choir and Orchestra of the Vienna State Opera,
Felix Prohaska, cond. Bach Guild BG 555 (with
Magnificat in D).

No. 51, JAUCHZET GOTT IN ALLEN LANDEN

Leipzig, 1731 or 1732, for the Fifteenth Sunday after
Trinity or for general use. This is a brilliant work
with a very elaborate part for the soprano. Stich-
Randall, it seems to me, comes off best here. While
a little more dash and assurance would have been
desirable, she negotiates the difficult part with good
intonation and an attractive tone. The trumpet is
sometimes a bit too loud for her in the first aria, but
the balance between the two is better in the last.
Danco's performance is acceptable, but her intonation is a little less secure and the orchestra has a
somewhat coarser sound. Schwarzkopf sings the
three middle movements very nicely, but has a little
trouble with the coloratura in the final one. And
her conductor takes the first aria at a pace that turns
it into a wild scramble. Schwarzkopf, a game filly,
races grimly on, but she is breathing hard long
before they reach the stretch.
——Teresa Stich-Randall (s); Vienna State Opera
Orchestra, Anton Heiller, cond. BACH GUILD BG
546 (with Cantata No. 209).
——Suzanne Danco (s); Stuttgart Chamber Or-

chestra, Karl Münchinger, cond. LONDON LL 993 (with Cantata No. 202).

——Elisabeth Schwarzkopf (s); Philharmonia Orchestra, Peter Gellhorn, cond. COLUMBIA ML 4792 (with Cantata No. 82 and two arias from other cantatas).

No. 53, SCHLAGE DOCH, GEWUENSCHTE STUNDE

Leipzig, about 1730. There is considerable doubt whether this work, which consists only of an aria for alto with violins, violas, continuo, and bells, is authentic. There can be little doubt, however, about which of the two available recordings of this lovely piece is the superior. Although the Decca version is well played and its bells have a finer, rounder sound than Westminster's, its alto is far surpassed by Rössl-Majdan, whose singing here is very beautiful. The M-G-M disk was not at hand for comparison.

——Hilde Rössl-Majdan (a); Orchestra of the Vienna State Opera, Hermann Scherchen, cond. WESTMINSTER XWN 18392 (with Cantatas Nos. 54 and 170).

——Hildegard Hennecke (a); Chamber Orchestra of the Schola Cantorum Basiliensis, August Wenzinger, cond. DECCA DL 9619 (with Cantatas Nos. 189 and 200).

[——Herta Glaz (c); Chamber Ensemble, Izler Solomon, cond. M-G-M 3156 (with Pergolesi: *Salve*).]

No. 54, WIDERSTEHE DOCH DER SUENDE

Leipzig, around 1730. This brief work consists of two alto arias connected by a recitative. The first aria, depicting a struggle against sin, contains poignant dissonances over a resolute basic rhythm. The second is a remarkable fugue on a partially chromatic subject. Beautifully sung by Rössl-Majdan. Since the work was probably performed by a male alto in Bach's time, Deller's remarkable countertenor no doubt provides the right vocal color. One wishes it had more variety and intensity here, especially in the recitatives, which proceed in a uniformly calm mood.

——Hilde Rössl-Majdan (a); Orchestra of the Vienna State Opera, Hermann Scherchen, cond. WESTMINSTER XWN 18392 (with Cantatas Nos. 53 and 170).

——Alfred Deller (c-t); Leonhardt Baroque Ensemble, Gustave Leonhardt, cond. BACH GUILD BG 550 (with Cantata No. 170).

No. 56, ICH WILL DEN KREUZSTAB GERNE TRAGEN

Leipzig, 1731 or 1732, for the Nineteenth Sunday after Trinity. A great work for solo bass, comprising a big, poignant aria, a joyful one, two very expressive accompanied recitatives, and a final chorale. The difficult solo part is handled rather well by both singers, but young Fischer-Dieskau is easily the superior by virtue of his firmer intonation. He has an annoying way (shared by many German singers though not by Pernerstorfer here) of sometimes separating the tones of a melisma on one syllable ("tra-ha-ha-ha-gen"), even though an oboe, say, has just shown him the proper phrasing. But his tone is rich and round, and he sings with the necessary fervor. The Bach Guild recording has a rather tubby bass, and there were clicks toward the end of the review disk.

——Dietrich Fischer-Dieskau (b); Berlin Motet Singers; Ristenpart Chamber Orchestra, Karl Ristenpart, cond. ARCHIVE ARC 3058 (with Cantata No. 82).

——Alois Pernerstorfer (bs); Vienna Symphony Orchestra and Chamber Choir, Jonathan Sternberg, cond. BACH GUILD BG 502 (with Cantata No. 34).

No. 57, SELIG IST DER MANN

Leipzig, about 1740, for the second day of Christmas. A kind of extended dialogue between Jesus (bass) and the Soul (soprano). The chorus enters only for the final chorale. This work is on the whole rather routine, for Bach, only the first soprano aria (No. 3) rising above that level. The performance is a bit stodgy, the soloists unexciting, and the recording mediocre. In the chorale the chorus is blurred and the pitch wavers.

——Agnes Giebel (s); Bruno Müller (bs); Pro Musica Orchestra and Chorus (Stuttgart), Rolf Reinhardt, cond. VOX PL 7340 (with Cantata No. 32).

No. 60, O EWIGKEIT, DU DONNERWORT

Leipzig, 1732, for the Twenty-fourth Sunday after Trinity. Another dialogue cantata, this time between Fear (alto) and Hope (tenor). In the opening duet, the most extensive piece in the work, the tenor's elaborate periods twine about the phrases of the chorale sung by the alto. As in the other cantatas in this album, the soloists sing acceptably but sound rather subdued. The orchestral tone is beautiful. Oboi d'amore are employed here, but the continuo is played on a piano.

——Carol Smith (a); Jan Peerce (t); Norman Farrow (bs); Chorus and Orchestra, Frank Brieff, cond. Two 12-in. RCA Victor lm 6023 (with Cantatas Nos. 41 and 42, and arias and duets from other cantatas).

No. 63, Christen, aetzet diesen Tag

Composed possibly at Halle in 1713, for the first day of Christmas. A fine work, predominantly jubilant in mood. No. 5 ("Praise the Lord with song and dancing"), a duet between alto and tenor in a minuetlike rhythm, –is especially delightful. The chorus has a few uncertain spots in No. 1 but sings very well when it returns in the last movement. Of the soloists, only the alto (in No. 2) and the tenor (in No. 4) rise above the ordinary. In No. 3, a duet for soprano and bass, the soprano is much too loud and the continuo proceeds on leaden feet.

——Margit Opawsky (s); Hilde Rössl-Majdan (a); Waldemar Kmentt (t); Harald Hermann (bs); Vienna Chamber Choir and State Orchestra, Michael Gielen, cond. Bach Guild bg 518.

No. 65, Sie werden aus Saba alle kommen

Leipzig, about 1724, for Epiphany. The crown of this work is the great opening chorus, depicting the procession of Wise Men and others bringing gold and frankincense to the Child. The altos are rather weak here. In the arias the bass exhibits excellent breath control and the tenor somewhat defective German pronunciation. The spirit of adoration is nicely conveyed by Roger Wagner. Flutes are used instead of recorders, but this is not too serious here. What is serious is the occasional wavering in intensity in the recording.

——Robert Sands (t); Ralph Isbell (bs); Roger Wagner Chorale and Chamber Orchestra, Roger Wagner, cond. LYRICHORD LL 50 (with Cantata No. 106).

No. 67, HALT' IM GEDAECHTNIS JESUM CHRIST

Leipzig, between 1723 and 1727, for the First Sunday after Easter. A fine work of which the high point is the great "aria" for bass and chorus. Unfortunately, the performance is stodgy, the chorus unclear, and the soloists undistinguished except for the alto, who, however, has only a few measures of recitative. In the bass "aria" the sound of the chorus twice suddenly fades. The work is sung in English and no text is provided.

——Kathleen Ferrier (a); William Herbert (t); William Parsons (bs); Cantata Singers; Jacques Orchestra, Reginald Jacques, cond. LONDON LL 845 (with Cantata No. 11 and *Jesu, Joy of Man's Desiring* from Cantata No. 147).

No. 70, WACHET, BETET

Revised at Leipzig in 1723 for the Twenty-sixth Sunday after Trinity, from a cantata composed at Weimar in 1716. One of Bach's masterworks, with a splendid opening chorus, a fine aria for each of the soloists, and two chorales, of which the first (No. 7) is especially beautiful. The high points are the dramatic accompanied recitative for bass, with the trumpet slashing through the orchestra with the tones of a chorale, and the following bass aria, its lovely flow interrupted by the exciting vision of the Day of Judgment (Nos. 9 and 10). The tempos are convincing and the chorus sings acceptably, but of the soloists only the soprano and the bass rise above the ordinary.

——Anny Felbermayer (s); Erika Wien (a); Hugo Meyer Welfing (t); Norman Foster (bs); Choir of the Bach Guild; Vienna State Opera Orchestra, Felix Prohaska, cond. Bach Guild bg 524.

No. 76, Die Himmel erzaehlen die Ehre Gottes

Leipzig, 1723, for the Second Sunday after Trinity. A magnificent work maintaining throughout its considerable length the exalted standard set in the opening movement. Most of the inner sections have a delicate chamber-music quality. The wonderfully expressive chorale that closes Part I is repeated at the end of Part II. All of the soloists are satisfactory, the alto and the unnamed trumpeter being especially good. The performance is imaginative, and the varying moods of the text are clearly conveyed. Highly recommended from every point of view.

——Magda Laszlo (s); Hilde Rössl-Majdan (a); Petre Munteanu (t); Richard Standen (bs); Akademiechor; Orchestra of the Vienna State Opera, Hermann Scherchen, cond. Westminster xwn 18393 (with Cantata No. 84).

No. 78, Jesu, der du meine Seele

Leipzig, between 1735 and 1744, for the Fourteenth Sunday after Trinity. One of the great cantatas, especially because of the extraordinarily moving opening chorus—a giant chorale fantasia on a chromatic descending bass—and the utterly delightful duet that follows. The continuo is rather boldly realized in this duet, but the result is effective. All of the soloists are competent, even though the bass does not have the most appealing tone conceivable. The chorus sounds better in loud passages than in soft, and is clearer in the first movement than in the last.

——Teresa Stich-Randall (s); Dagmar Hermann (a); Anton Dermota (t); Hans Braun (bs); Choir and Orchestra of the Bach Guild, Felix Prohaska, cond. BACH GUILD BG 537 (with Cantata No. 106).

No. 79, GOTT, DER HERR

Leipzig, possibly in 1735, for the Reformation Festival. The magnificent opening chorus, resplendent with horns and drums, and a fine duet for soprano and bass are the high spots of this work imbued with sturdy faith. The vocal soloists are adequate and the chorus acceptable, although its sound in the first movement could have been clearer. Whether this is a fault of the singing or of the otherwise satisfactory recording I cannot say. A special word of praise is in order for the unnamed players of the difficult horn parts.

——Gunthild Weber (s); Lore Fischer (a); Hermann Schey (bs); Berlin Motet Choir; Berlin Philharmonic Orchestra, Fritz Lehmann, cond. ARCHIVE ARC 3065 (with Cantata No. 19).

No. 80, EIN' FESTE BURG IST UNSER GOTT

Leipzig, 1730, or 1739, for the Reformation Festival, in the version that has survived. In this very elaborate work Bach employs the melody of the celebrated chorale in four of the movements. It is a powerful and dramatic composition that belongs near the top of Bach's vocal music. The unnamed soloists are adequate and the chorus only fair. In the highly contrapuntal opening movement the melodic lines are not always clearly drawn by the chorus.

——Soloists; Akademiechor; Vienna Chamber Orchestra, Felix Prohaska, cond. BACH GUILD BG 508.

No. 82, ICH HABE GENUG

Leipzig, mostly in 1731 or 1732, for the Purification of Mary. A solo cantata consisting of three arias and two recitatives. Two of the arias, *Ich habe genug* and *Schlummert ein*, are very beautiful. Both Hotter and Fischer-Dieskau have fine voices— Hotter's is slightly darker in color—and sing expressively here. Fischer-Dieskau's trill needs more work; Hotter usually contents himself with a single turn. The Columbia recording seems older; the sound is two-dimensional, so to speak, whereas in the Archive the voice stands out in relief.

——Hans Hotter (bar); Philharmonia Orchestra, Anthony Bernard, cond. COLUMBIA ML 4792 (with Cantata No. 51 and two arias from other cantatas).

——Dietrich Fischer-Dieskau (bar); Berlin Motet Singers; Ristenpart Chamber Orchestra, Karl Ristenpart, cond. ARCHIVE ARC 3058 (with Cantata No. 56).

No. 84, ICH BIN VERGNUEGT

Leipzig, 1731 or 1732, for Septuagesima. This cantata consists of two arias and two recitatives for soprano and a final chorale. It was written, according to Spitta, to be sung by Anna Magdalena Bach at domestic performances in the Bach household. It is a cheerful work and Laszlo sings it pleasantly, although her top notes are not always firmly focused. No printed text is supplied.

——Magda Laszlo (s); Akademiechor; Orchestra of the Vienna State Opera, Hermann Scherchen, cond. WESTMINSTER XWN 18393 (with Cantata No. 76).

No. 104, DU HIRTE ISRAEL, HOERE

Leipzig, between 1723 and 1727, for the Second Sunday after Easter. The tender lyricism that permeates this pastoral work makes it one of the loveliest idyls among the cantatas. Cuenod as usual turns in a good performance. Pernerstorfer's voice has a pleasant quality here, but he seldom hits a note in dead center. The chorus is adequate although the tenors are rather weak and they and the sopranos sometimes sound a little quavery.

——Hugues Cuenod (t); Alois Pernerstorfer (bs); Vienna Chamber Choir and Symphony Orchestra, Jonathan Sternberg, cond. BACH GUILD BG 503 (with Cantata No. 46).

No. 105, HERR, GEHE NICHT IN'S GERICHT

Leipzig, between 1723 and 1727, for the Ninth Sunday after Trinity. One of the great cantatas, unusually dramatic and intense, sustaining its high level of inspiration and imagination from the first measure to the last. The choral balance is excellent and the work of the soloists acceptable. Lehmann does not quite get out of this work everything that is in it. The horn in the tenor aria avoids the notes above the staff and plays an octave lower in such passages. There are no bands between movements, and the envelope supplies only an English translation of the text. But this is one case where a less than perfect presentation is far better than none at all.

——Gunthild Weber (s); Lore Fischer (a); Helmut Krebs (t); Hermann Schey (bs); Berlin Motet Choir; Berlin Philharmonic Orchestra, Fritz Lehmann, cond. ARCHIVE ARC 3066 (with Cantata No. 39).

No. 106, GOTTES ZEIT IST DIE ALLERBESTE ZEIT (ACTUS TRAGICUS)

This great funeral cantata, one of Bach's early choral works (it may have been composed at Mühlhausen in 1707), is also one of his most popular. The Lyrichord version, despite the round, firm tone of the chorus and the high quality of the bass soloist, must be ranked last, chiefly because of the surface noise and the distortion near the center of the disk. The Westminster performance is highly polished, although I am not sure that Scherchen's use of a bouncy staccato for animated eighth-note passages suits this music. He has, however, the advantage of a first-rate alto. Prohaska's instrumentation is more authentic (recorders and organ as against Scherchen's flutes and harpsichord); his soloists are fair; and his interpretation is effective in its more matter-of-fact and straightforward way.

——Dagmar Hermann (a); Hans Braun (bs); Choir and Baroque Ensemble of the Bach Guild, Felix Prohaska, cond. BACH GUILD BG 537 (with Cantata No. 78).

——Hilde Rössl-Majdan (a); Alfred Poell (bs); Akademiechor; Orchestra of the Vienna State

Opera, Hermann Scherchen, cond. WESTMINSTER
XWN 18394 (with Cantata No. 140).
——Katherine Hilgenberg (a); Ralph Isbell (bs);
Roger Wagner Chorale and Chamber Orchestra,
Roger Wagner, cond. LYRICHORD LL 50 (with Cantata No. 65).

No. 122, DAS NEUGEBOR'NE KINDELEIN

Leipzig, about 1742, for the Sunday after Christmas. The cheerful opening chorus and a fine trio
for soprano, alto, and tenor, with the alto singing
the chorale melody, are the outstanding movements here. The soloists are adequate. While the
bass's tones could be more firmly focused, he sings
Bach's cruelly long phrases with apparent ease.
There was some crackling on the review disk in his
recitative.
——Margit Opawsky (s); Hilde Rössl-Majdan a);
Waldemar Kmentt (t); Harald Hermann (bs);
Vienna Chamber Choir; Vienna State Opera Orchestra, Michael Gielen, cond. BACH GUILD BG 523
(with Cantata No. 133).

No. 131, AUS DER TIEFE

Composed at Mühlhausen, probably in 1707. This
cantata, one of the earliest of Bach's that have
come down to us, is an exceptionally fine work.
Some writers, beginning with Spitta, feel that the
choral writing is sometimes too instrumental in
character, but it is surely no more so than in many
later cantatas. The composition consists of three
choral movements separated by two arias, one for
bass and the other for tenor. In the course of the
elaborate bass aria a soprano sings some lines of

the chorale; and an alto does the same in the tenor aria. In both cases Shaw uses several sopranos and altos instead of one—probably a legitimate, and in any case an effective, procedure. The soloists are satisfactory, and the tone of both chorus and orchestra is very beautiful. My disk has some annoying crackles at the beginning. No text is supplied.

——William Hess (t); Paul Matthen (bs); Robert Shaw Chorale; RCA Victor Orchestra, Robert Shaw, cond. RCA Victor lm 1100 (with Cantata No. 140).

No. 133, Ich freue mich in dir

Leipzig, 1735 or 1737, for the third day of Christmas. The delightfully gay chorus at the beginning and a lovely aria for soprano stand out here. All the soloists are satisfactory, the soprano and bass, particularly, singing with somewhat more assurance than in No. 122. Some crackles here too, in the alto aria.

——Margit Opawsky (s); Hilde Rössl-Majdan (a); Waldemar Kmentt (t); Harald Hermann (bs); Vienna Chamber Choir; Vienna State Opera Orchestra, Michael Gielen, cond. Bach Guild bg 523 (with Cantata No. 122).

No. 137, Lobe den Herren, den maechtigen Koenig

Leipzig, 1732 or later, for the Twelfth Sunday after Trinity. The high spots in this work are the first chorus, with its lyric and quietly joyful subject, and the duet for soprano and bass, with its expressive chromatic lines. The performance is nothing to cheer about: the chorus and solo soprano, alto, and tenor are adequate, the bass somewhat better. The trumpets are too loud in both of the choral movements and not always on pitch. The recording itself is very clear in the two arias and the duet, less so in the choral numbers.

——Claire Fassbender-Luz (s); Hetty Plümacher (a); Claus Stemann (t); Bruno Müller (bs); Stuttgart Choral Society; Stuttgart Bach Orchestra, Hans Grischkat, cond. RENAISSANCE X 37 (with Cantata No. 9).

No. 140, WACHET AUF

Leipzig, 1731 or 1742, for the Twenty-seventh Sunday after Trinity. Perhaps the best known of Bach's cantatas, this masterwork handles the three verses of the chorale in three different ways: 1) in a great and colorful movement for chorus and orchestra, the chorale tune being sung by the sopranos; 2) in a movement where a wonderful new melody in the upper strings winds itself around the sturdy old chorale, sung by unison tenors (this movement was later made into an organ chorale-prelude by Bach and that version in turn became popular in Busoni's transcription for piano); and 3) in a straight four-part setting for chorus and orchestra. The three verses are separated each time by a recitative and duet.

The choice, it seems to me, lies between the Scherchen and Shaw versions. Prohaska's performance is pretty good, but the sound of his chorus is not so clear as in the other two recordings; his recitatives are rather prosaic; the bass in the first duet is somewhat too far back; and there is some distortion on high notes in the second verse and in the final movement. Shaw's chorus provides the most beautiful tone. He takes the first movement rather fast, apparently following Schweitzer's view that it depicts the confusion attendant upon the cry "Awake!" The oboes are rather faint here; in fact, the whole Victor recording seems to have been made at a low dynamic level, but the chorus comes through clearly. In the second verse the tenors are rather superfluously doubled by a trumpet not indicated in the score; and in the second duet the naked bass is played, the figures not being realized. There were some crackles on the review disk. No text is supplied by Victor. Scherchen seems to agree with Schering that the first movement represents a solemn procession and consequently plays it a little more slowly than Shaw. The choral balance is as good as in the Victor though the oboes here, too, are too faint. The review disk contained some clicks at the beginning.

The soloists in all three performances are acceptable. In each, an ordinary violin is used instead of the violino piccolo Bach asks for in the first duet. If I had to choose, I think I would take the Scherchen, chiefly because of its greater authenticity.

——Magda Laszlo (s); Waldemar Kmentt (t); Alfred Poell (bs); Akademiechor; Orchestra of the Vienna State Opera, Hermann Scherchen, cond. WESTMINSTER XWN 18394 (with Cantata No. 106).
——S. Freil (s); R. Russell (t); P. Matthen (bs); Robert Shaw Chorale; RCA Victor Orchestra, Robert Shaw, cond. RCA VICTOR LM 1100 (with Cantata No. 131).

——Anny Felbermayer (s); Alfred Uhl (t); Hans Braun (bs); Choir and Orchestra of the Bach Guild, Felix Prohaska, cond. BACH GUILD BG 511 (with Cantata No. 4).

No. 146, WIR MUESSEN DURCH VIEL TRUEBSAL

Leipzig, about 1740, for the Third Sunday after Easter. The superb *sinfonia*, with its elaborate organ part, is a transcription of the first movement of the Clavier Concerto in D minor, and the moving chorus that follows is superimposed on material from the slow movement of the same concerto. The authenticity of this work has been challenged, but it is hard to imagine that anyone else could have created new choral music of this caliber that would fit so perfectly with the borrowed instrumental music. The beautiful soprano aria and the rousing duet for tenor and bass are also out of Bach's top drawer. Prohaska's performance is spirited and the soloists are acceptable. Felbermayer, indeed, is a good deal more than that: she is at the top of her form here, singing with lovely quality and very musically. The chorus sounds a little remote, as compared with the organ, in the second movement but the balance elsewhere is first-rate. There were some crackles on the review disk.

——Anny Felbermayer, (s); Erika Wien (a); Hugo Meyer Welfing (t); Norman Foster (bs); Choir of the Bach Guild; Vienna State Opera Orchestra, Felix Prohaska, cond. BACH GUILD BG 525.

No. 152, TRITT AUF DIE GLAUBENSBAHN

Weimar, perhaps in 1714, for the Sunday after Christmas. This tender and happy work is written for solo soprano and bass, with recorder, oboe, viola d'amore, viola da gamba, and continuo, here played on an organ. The intimate character of the music is well conveyed by Haas and by the excellent recording. The tone of the recorder is rather nasal, and it consequently matches the astringent tone of the other instruments in the *sinfonia*, but a rounder and purer recorder sound would have been more suitable in the soprano aria. This is acceptably sung by Miss Bond, who can command a real trill. Irwin has a clear, true baritone voice that is very pleasant to hear. The review disk contains some crackles in his aria. No text is supplied. ——Dorothy Bond (s); Robert Irwin (bar); London Baroque Ensemble, Karl Haas, cond. WESTMINSTER XWN 18391 (with Cantata No. 32).

No. 161, KOMM, DU SUESSE TODESSTUNDE

Weimar, probably 1715, for the Sixteenth Sunday after Trinity. A lovely work, full of sweetness and fervor. The great chorale *Herzlich tut mich verlangen*, familiar from its use in the St. *Matthew Passion*, appears here twice—as a countermelody played by the organ in the alto's first aria and as the final movement, performed by chorus and orchestra. The tenor can sing a very long phrase on one breath, but his intonation is not always as precise as it should be. Rössl-Majdan, as usual, sings beautifully. Some surface noise at the beginning. ——Hilde Rössl-Majdan (a); Waldemar Kmentt (t); Choir and Orchestra of the Bach Guild, Felix Prohaska, cond. BACH GUILD BG 513 (with Cantata No. 202).

No. 170, VERGNUEGTE RUH'

Leipzig, 1731 or 1732, for the Sixth Sunday after Trinity. This appealing work consists of three arias and two recitatives for alto, obbligato organ, strings, and oboe d'amore (doubling the first violin throughout). Each of the three recordings available for evaluation has its merits and defects. Lehmann's graver tempos in the first and last arias seem better suited to the text, and his organist plays with skill and tasteful registration. Scherchen uses a harpsichord instead of an organ, and in the first and second arias his soloist is not far enough forward. But the decisive point is the quality of the singing; and here, it seems to me, there is no question about the relative inferiority of Höngen. She sings with feeling, but her voice is unsteady, and this is particularly noticeable in the second aria, where the voice is one instrument among several of equal importance. Both Rössl-Majdan and Deller sing extremely well here. I find the lady's voice warmer and more varied in color. In the review copy of the Bach Guild disk there were defective grooves at the beginning.

——Hilde Rössl-Majdan (a); Orchestra of the Vienna State Opera, Hermann Scherchen, cond. WESTMINSTER WL 5197 (with Contatas Nos. 53 and 54).

——Alfred Deller (c-t); Leonhardt Baroque Ensemble, Gustav Leonhardt, cond. BACH GUILD BG 550 (with Cantata No. 54).

——Elisabeth Höngen (a); Bavarian State Orchestra, Fritz Lehmann, cond. ARCHIVE ARC 3067 (with Cantata No. 189).

[——Herta Glaz (c); Chamber Ensemble, Izler Solomon, cond. M-G-M 3156.]

No. 189, MEINE SEELE RUEHMT UND PREIST

According to some scholars, this is an early work, written between 1707 and 1710; Spitta places it late in the Leipzig period; still others doubt that it is authentic. It consists of three arias and two recitatives and is, in the present writer's opinion, a rather routine work, for Bach. Both tenors perform it satisfactorily, Schiøtz's voice sounding somewhat drier than Ludwig's here. The Columbia recording, which was made at the Casals Festival in Perpignan, employs a flute instead of a recorder and provides only a partial translation of the text. The Archive uses the recorder and supplies German text and English translation.

——Walther Ludwig (t); Chamber Orchestra, Fritz Lehmann, cond. ARCHIVE ARC 3067 (with Cantata No. 170).

——Aksel Schiøtz (t); John Wummer (fl); Marcel Tabuteau (ob); Alexander Schneider (vn); Paul Tortelier (vcl); Robert Veyron-Lacroix (hpscd). COLUMBIA ML 4641 (with Beethoven: *An die ferne Geliebte*).

No. 198, TRAUER-ODE

Composed at Leipzig in 1727 on the death of Christiane Eberhardine, Queen of Poland and Electress of Saxony. The version recorded here is the original *Funeral Ode*, not the one with a new text for All Saints' Day and added chorales, made by Wilhelm Rust in the nineteenth century. Bach himself used some of this music in 1731 for his

St. Mark Passion, now lost. It is easy to see why he did so: the *Trauer-Ode* contains some magnificent music, especially in the three choral movements; and there is a charming bit of tone painting in the representation of bells in the brief alto recitative. Scherchen molds the choral phrases beautifully, the continuo does not drag, and the soloists are all satisfactory. There is some surface noise.

——Magda Laszlo (s); Hilde Rössl-Majdan (a); Waldemar Kmentt (t); Alfred Poell (bs); Akademiechor; Orchestra of the Vienna State Opera, Hermann Scherchen, cond. WESTMINSTER XWN 18395.

No. 200, BEKENNEN WILL ICH SEINEN NAMEN

This is an aria for alto, violins, and continuo that is thought to be a fragment of a cantata. It was first published in 1935. It is not an important piece, and the soloist is barely adequate.

——Hildegard Hennecke (a); Chamber Orchestra of the Schola Cantorum Basiliensis, August Wenzinger, cond. DECCA DL 9619 (with Cantatas Nos. 53 and 189).

No. 201, DER STREIT ZWISCHEN PHOEBUS UND PAN

This secular cantata was written by Bach for performance by the Collegium Musicum at Leipzig in 1731. It depicts a contest between Phoebus, who represents lofty and serious music, and Pan, who stands for light, easily understandable music. It is Phoebus, of course, who wins; and Pan's adherent,

Midas, is crowned with asses' ears. Yet in the
music allotted to Pan, he is not given all the worst
of it; in fact, the middle section of his test aria
contains an amusing burlesque of the serious style.
In the character of Midas, Bach is said to have
intended a caricature of a young Leipzig critic of
his, so that we have here a musical precedent for
Wagner's Beckmesser-Hanslick. While the parody
is rather mild, to modern ears, the work contains
a good deal of gaiety and charm. The chorus comes
through more clearly in the Bach Guild version.
The soloists in that performance are more satisfactory on the whole: its Pan (Wolfram) and
Momus (Schlemm) are superior to the performers
of those parts in the Renaissance recording (Kelch
and Nentwig); both Phoebuses, Midases, and
Tmoluses are more or less equally good; and only
the Renaissance Mercurius (Michaelis) is better
than her counterpart on Bach Guild (Eustrati). A
clear advantage of the latter version is the flexibility
of the recitatives; Grischkat's singers perform them
as though to a metronome. Neither recording is
free from surface noise, and the trumpeters in both
have difficulty with the pitch.

——Anny Schlemm (s); Diana Eustrati (a); Gert
Lutze (t); Herbert Reinhold (t); Gerhard Niese
(bs); Karl Wolfram (bs); Choir and Orchestra
of the Bach Guild, Helmut Koch, cond. BACH
GUILD BG 514.

——Käthe Nentwig (s); Ruth Michaelis (a);
Werner Hohmann (t); Alfred Pfeifle (t); Bruno
Müller (bs); Franz Kelch (bs); Swabian Choral
Singers; Tonstudio Orchestra (Stuttgart), Hans
Grischkat, cond. RENAISSANCE X 42.

No. 202, WEICHET NUR, BETRUEBTE SCHATTEN
(WEDDING CANTATA)

Composed probably in Cöthen (1717-1723). A tender and intimate work for soprano, oboe, strings, and continuo. Both singers handle the long curves of the phrases well. Danco's voice, as reproduced here, is richer and more sensuous but occasionally reveals a slight tremolo, of which Felbermayer's is free. More appealing singing in the London disk; steadier, if perhaps less interesting, singing in the Bach Guild. The continuo in the latter, played by harpsichord and bass, is a little thumpy.

——Suzanne Danco (s); Stuttgart Chamber Orchestra, Karl Münchinger, cond. LONDON LL 993 (with Cantata No. 51).

——Anny Felbermayer (s); Orchestra of the Bach Guild, Felix Prohaska, cond. BACH GUILD BG 513 (with Cantata No. 161).

No. 203, AMORE TRADITORE

Leipzig, about 1735. This is one of two surviving cantatas with Italian texts that are attributed to Bach. It is for bass voice with harpsichord accompaniment, the only one of Bach's cantatas for such a combination, and consists of two *da capo* arias separated by a recitative. Its authenticity has been questioned. Müller, normally a dependable singer, does not seem happy with this dull work.

——Bruno Müller (bs); Helma Elsner, harpsichord. Vox PL 8980 (with Cantata No. 211).

No. 205, DER ZUFRIEDENGESTELLTE AEOLUS

This dramatic cantata was written at Leipzig in 1725 to celebrate the nameday of August Friedrich

Müller, a professor of philosophy at the university there. The performance is said to have been intended to take place out of doors, and the orchestration of certain movements—for example, Aeolus' aria with trumpets, horns, drums, and continuo only—is adduced as evidence. One wonders, however, how such an aria as Zephyrus' (with viola d'amore, viola da gamba, and continuo) or Pallas' (with solo violin and continuo) would sound in the open air. In any case, I cannot imagine a Ph.D. who would not feel honored by a birthday gift like this, for Bach, as usual, poured fine ideas and impeccable workmanship into this occasional piece. The music may seem a bit heavy at times for its purpose, but the general mood is rather gay.

Neither performance is completely satisfactory. Grischkat favors slower tempos, and his tenor has to break a long phrase in half in his aria. As in most of this conductor's cantata recordings, the recitatives are too regular in rhythm. The operatic accompanied recitative for Aeolus (No. 2) comes out flat and lacking in dramatic interest. The chorus has a thinner sound. In the first movement the sopranos have trouble with notes above the staff. The tenor (Zephyrus) sings the high notes of his gentle aria in falsetto, apparently as a matter of "interpretation," because he does not do so in his duet with the alto (No. 13). Both the soprano and the alto sing acceptably, though the former's top tones are rather pale. The first trumpet has some difficulty with the pitch in his cruelly high part. Only the bass, singing the important part of Aeolus, is superior to his opposite number. Koch's performance has more imagination and vivacity. The sound of his chorus, which is clearer in the last movement than in the first, is generally rounder. Three of his vocal soloists and his first trumpet are better. His Aeolus, unfortunately, seldom strikes a tone squarely in the middle, and the pitches of the high notes in his wide-ranging part are very approximate indeed. This recording contains less surface noise than the Renaissance.

——Anny Schlemm (s); Diana Eustrati (a); Gert Lutze (t); Karl Wolfram (bs); Choir and Orchestra of the Bach Guild, Helmut Koch, cond. BACH GUILD BG 515.

——Käthe Nentwig (s); Ruth Michaelis (a); Werner Hohmann (t); Franz Kelch (bs); Swabia Choral Singers; Tonstudio Orchestra (Stuttgart), Hans Grischkat, cond. RENAISSANCE X 43.

No. 209, NON SA CHE SIA DOLORE

Leipzig, between 1730 and 1734. This is considerably superior to No. 203, the other surviving Italian cantata by Bach. It is scored for flute, strings, and continuo. Beginning with an interesting *sinfonia*, it continues with a rather melancholy recitative and aria, and concludes with a fine and optimistic aria. A little more bravura would be welcome in this final movement, but Stich-Randall sings throughout with a firm, pure tone.

——Teresa Stich-Randall (s); Vienna State Opera Orchestra, Anton Heiller, cond. BACH GUILD BG 546 (with Cantata No. 51).

No. 210, O HOLDER TAG, ERWUENSCHTE ZEIT (WEDDING CANTATA)

Leipzig, probably about 1734-1735. A gentle and very lyric cantata for soprano with flute, oboe d'amore, strings, and continuo, consisting of five recitatives

and as many arias. Laszlo's voice is pleasant, and she handles her difficult part, with its two-octave range, with a good deal of skill. While the arias vary in rhythm and texture, this is a long work. Because of the regular alternation of recitative and aria and the persistence of an *andante* basic pulse almost throughout, it is perhaps advisable to listen to it in sections, which is the way it was undoubtedly performed originally, probably between courses of a wedding feast. There is some surface noise.
——Magda Laszlo (s); Orchestra of the Vienna State Opera, Hermann Scherchen, cond. WESTMINSTER XWN 18396.

No. 211, SCHWEIGT STILLE, PLAUDERT NICHT (COFFEE CANTATA)

The "Coffee" Cantata composed at Leipzig about 1732, is about as close as Bach ever got to writing opera—and comic opera at that. The wisp of a "plot" concerns an eighteenth-century teen-ager's addiction to the insidious product of the roasted bean and her father's anxious attempt to cure her of that vice. Bach, characteristically, handled it as carefully as though the text were important, and the music is not easy to perform. It is nicely sung here, with the proper tongue-in-cheek solemnity.
——Friederike Sailer (s); Johannes Feyerabend (t); Bruno Müller (bs); Pro Musica Orchestra (Stuttgart), Rolf Reinhardt, cond. VOX PL 8980 (with Cantata No. 203).

MOTETS

Six Motets, S. 225-230

An excellent job. The chorus of St. Thomas's in Leipzig sings with good tone and balance. It is apparently all male, the treble parts being sung by boys. Some of these magnificent works may be had in more exciting performances (*see below*), but the present readings all have solid values, not the least of which are the clarity of the contrapuntal sections, the faithful representation of the varying moods of the music, and Ramin's plastic phrasing.
——Thomanerchor, Leipzig, Günther Ramin, dir. Two 12-in. Archive arc 3040/41.

Singet dem Herrn ein neues Lied, S. 225

Composed for two four-part choruses, possibly for New Year's Day 1746, to celebrate the conclusion of the second Silesian War. What Hindemith accomplishes with the Yale students is nothing short of a minor miracle. They sing this excruciatingly difficult piece with fantastic verve, complete surety, and attractive tone quality. Each line is given its proper place in the musical scheme; the performance never degenerates into an undifferentiated mass of sound. It is too bad that we don't have more Bach conducted by Hindemith on records. Grossmann's performance, which is in the conventional style, is acceptable, though in harmonically complicated passages of the first section the

intonation is not always certain or the texture clear.
——Collegium Musicum, School of Music, Yale University, Paul Hindemith, cond. OVERTONE LR 4 (with works by Monteverdi, Weelkes, and Gesualdo).
——Thomanerchor, on ARCHIVE ARC 3040.
——Vienna Akademie Kammerchor, Ferdinand Grossmann, cond. 12-in. WESTMINSTER XWN 18205 (with *Jesu meine Freude* and *Komm, Jesu, komm*).

JESU MEINE FREUDE, S. 227

A funeral motet, composed at Leipzig in 1723. This expressive and powerful work is written for a five-part chorus. The crack Robert Shaw Chorale sings (in English) with fine balance, impeccable intonation, and beautiful tone. Shaw brings out the drama in the fifth movement and the tenderness in the poignant ninth movement, but elsewhere there is a somewhat impersonal air about his interpretation. The Vienna chorus is not quite as efficient or as well blended, and there are moments of doubtful pitch, but otherwise this, too, is an acceptable reading. All three recordings reproduce the chorus with clarity and spaciousness. There is a higher level of surface noise on the Victor.
——Robert Shaw Chorale; RCA Victor Orchestra, Robert Shaw, cond. RCA VICTOR LM 9035 (with Cantata No. 4).
——Thomanerchor, on ARCHIVE ARC 3041.
——Vienna Akademie Kammerchor, Ferdinand Grossmann, cond. WESTMINSTER XWN 18205 (with *Komm, Jesu, komm* and *Singet dem Herrn ein neues Lied*).

Komm, Jesu, komm, S. 229

This gentle work was composed for two four-part choruses at Leipzig between 1723 and 1734. These are all competent performances. Victor is the only one that uses instrumental support—a legitimate procedure. Indeed, it seems probable that all of Bach's motets were performed in his time with at least keyboard accompaniment. The choice here will perhaps be determined by the other items on the same disk. Victor supplies English text only; Archive only German; Westminster German and English.

——Vienna Akademie Kammerchor, Ferdinand Grossmann, cond. WESTMINSTER xwn 18205 (with *Jesu meine Freude* and *Singet dem Herrn ein neues Lied*).

——Thomanerchor, on ARCHIVE arc 3041.

——Robert Shaw Chorale; String Ensemble; Robert Shaw, cond. RCA VICTOR lm 1784 (with Schubert: Mass in G; Brahms: Three Songs).

THE MASSES, SANCTUS AND MAGNIFICAT

Mass in B Minor

It is very difficult to choose among the top four. Karajan and Scherchen have a more imaginative approach, but the former is likely to maintain a tempo-and-dynamic scheme doggedly throughout a movement; the latter, while keeping a steady basic pulse, achieves more nuance above it. Karajan's choral tenors are a bit weak, especially in the *Gratias agimus tibi* (No. 6) and the *Qui tollis* (No. 8), but otherwise his chorus has a fine, clear sound. He is favored with the best soprano of the group—Schwarzkopf, whose *Laudamus te* (No. 5) is a particular joy to hear. None of his other soloists is less than satisfactory, though the tenor sings better in the duet, *Domine Deus* (No. 7), than in the aria, *Benedictus* (No. 22). One might disagree with a few details of Karajan's interpretation—for example, the *Cum sancto Spiritu* (No. 11) is rather bouncy and the great Agnus Dei somewhat slow—but many of the other movements are extremely well done, such as the wonderfully joyous *Et in terra* (No. 4) and the deeply moving *Et incarnatus est* (No. 15). The instrumental balances are excellent, except in the *Qui tollis*, where the first flute is too loud. The surfaces are the least noisy of the lot. The sound here is clean and resonant but recorded at a low level (especially side 3), so that the volume has to be turned up, particularly for the solo portions.

Scherchen's chorus does not seem to have any weak spots. If it is blurred in the *Et resurrexit* (No. 17), the fault is the conductor's, who takes this movement so fast that the triplet figure cannot be articulated clearly. Elsewhere, however, the choral lines are pure and flexible. Scherchen takes the giant choral fugue of the Kyrie more slowly and broadly than his colleagues, but builds it up to a most imposing structure. His solo soprano is first-rate (though she does not have quite the warmth or the breath control of Schwarzkopf) and the other soloists are almost as good. This is an intelligent and musical performance. With respect to balance, "presence," and clarity in general, the recording is excellent, though not new.

Shaw does not come out badly in the face of such stiff competition. His performing forces are on the same level of competence, his chorus, solo bass (Matthen), and solo violinist (Oscar Shumsky) being in some respects even better. It is in the matter of penetration into the essence of the music that he sometimes does not quite come up to Karajan and Scherchen. The second soprano is a little weak in the *Christe* (No. 2) and in various passages the sound is rather bottom-heavy. This is the only recording of the Mass in which the *Osanna* is not repeated, as it should be, after the *Benedictus*. But by and large this is a performance that is far above average and, considering that it appeared on 78s in pre-microgroove days, it is rather well recorded. No text is supplied.

Thomas's soloists are all good, and he achieves a just balance between chorus and orchestra (though not always within the chorus itself), but he favors slowish tempos, and his somewhat reserved approach seldom attains eloquence.

It will be noticed that the Bach Guild and Urania sets have the same soloists and conductor but list different choruses and orchestras. The Regent set presents an entirely different galaxy of performers (all unknown to the present writer). Now, if all three sets do not represent one and the same performance, I will eat my hat, or even listen again to the Respighi transcription of Bach's Passacaglia and Fugue. The only differences I could discern were that Bach Guild seemed to be recorded most clearly, that the pre-echo noticeable at the beginning of some of its movements disappears in the other two sets, and that Regent has the noisiest surfaces. It is not, on the whole, a bad performance, and the solo tenor is superior to his opposite numbers. But in view of the manifest superiority in most other respects of the Angel, Westminster, Victor, and Oiseau-Lyre sets, it does not seem worth while listing the defects of these.

——Elisabeth Schwarzkopf (s); Marga Höffgen (a); Nicolai Gedda (t); Heinz Rehfuss (bs); Chorus and Orchestra of the Society of the Friends of Music, Vienna, Herbert von Karajan, cond. Three 12-in. ANGEL 3500c.

——Emmy Loose (s); Hilde Ceska (s); Gertrud Burgsthaler-Schuster (a); Anton Dermota (t); Alfred Poell (bs); Akademie Kammerchor; Vienna Symphony Orchestra, Hermann Scherchen, cond. Three 12-in. WESTMINSTER WAL 301.

——Anne McKnight (s); June Gardner (s); Lydia Summers (a); Lucius Metz (t); Paul Matthen (bs); RCA Victor Chorale and Orchestra, Robert Shaw, cond. Three 12-in. RCA VICTOR LM 6100.

——Lisa Schwarzweller (s); Lore Fischer (a); Helmut Kretschmar (t); Bruno Müller (bs); Choir of the Dreikönigskirche, Frankfurt; Collegium Musicum Orchestra, Kurt Thomas, cond. Three 12-in. OISEAU-LYRE OL 50094/96.

——Gunthild Weber (s); Margherita de Landi (a); Helmut Krebs (t); Karl Wolfram (bs); Berlin Chamber Choirs; Berlin Symphony Orchestra, Fritz Lehmann, cond. Two 12-in. BACH GUILD BG 527/28.

——Gunthild Weber (s); Margherita de Landi (a);

Helmut Krebs (t); Karl Wolfram (bs); Chorus and Orchestra of Radio Berlin, Fritz Lehmann, cond. Two 12-in. URANIA URLP 236.

——Gerda Heidrich (s); Anita Brunner (a); Christian Bochner (t); Josef Kuntz (bs); Rhineland Symphony Orchestra, Alfred Federer, cond. Three 12-in. REGENT MG 6000.

SHORT MASSES AND SANCTUS

Each of the four short Masses consists of the Kyrie and Gloria only. The G major and G minor were put together entirely from music borrowed from earlier cantatas, and the other two consist largely of such borrowings. This is solid middle-grade Bach, the A major deserving perhaps a somewhat higher ranking than that. The four settings of the Sanctus have no connection with these Masses. They were written separately, apparently at different times. It is believed that only the D major was probably composed by Bach and that the other three may be his arrangements of works by other composers. Of these three the D minor is of considerable interest, no matter who wrote it. The performances are all on the routine side. The soloists are capable enough, but the conducting is relentlessly four-square. The instruments are often too loud in relation to the chorus.

——*Missa Brevis No. 1, in F; Sanctus No. 1, in C.* Agnes Giebel (s); Lotte Wolf-Matthäus (a); Franz Kelch (bs); Swabian Choral Singers; Tonstudio Orchestra (Stuttgart), Hans Grischkat, cond. RENAISSANCE X 44.

——*Missa Brevis No. II, in A; Sanctus No. II, in D.* Same as above. RENAISSANCE X 45.

——*Missa Brevis No. III, in G minor; Sanctus No. III, in D minor.* Lotte Wolf-Matthäus (a); Werner Hohmann (t); Franz Kelch (bs); Swabian Choral Singers; Tonstudio Orchestra (Stuttgart), Hans Grischkat, cond. RENAISSANCE X 46.

——*Missa Brevis No. IV, in G; Sanctus No. IV, in G.* Agnes Giebel (s); Lotte Wolf-Matthäus (a); Werner Hohmann (t); Franz Kelch (bs); Swabian Choral Singers; Tonstudio Orchestra (Stuttgart), Hans Grischkat, cond. RENAISSANCE X 47.

MAGNIFICAT

Leipzig, 1723. None of these recordings is a fully satisfactory representation of this splendid work. In all but one of them the faster movements jog along at a comfortable trot and the slow ones are equally unexciting. Prohaska's quick tempos are generally speedier than those of the other conductors, but he also goes in for a kind of bounciness that does not always suit the text. Only once, in Walter Reinhart's *Deposuit potentes*, are we offered a flash of the drama immanent in this magnificent music. Unfortunately, the rest of his performance is not up to the level of this movement; in fact, it is inferior in most respects to the other four. The soloists are best in the Bach Guild and the Vox, and the latter offers the most music for your money. The Magnificat exists in two versions—one in E-flat, with four additional Christmas movements as interpolations, and a later one in D, without the interpolations. All four recordings here are of the later version, but Vox adds the four earlier interpolations. No text is supplied by Concert Hall.

——Friederike Sailer (s); Lotte Wolf-Matthäus (a); Hetty Plümacher (a); Johannes Feyerabend (t); Bruno Müller (bs); Chorus of Radio Stuttgart; Pro Musica Orchestra, Rolf Reinhardt, cond. Vox PL 8890.

——Mimi Coertse, Margaret Sjöstedt (ss); Hilde Rössl-Majdan (a); Anton Dermota (t); Frederick Guthrie (bs); Choir and Orchestra of the Vienna State Opera, Felix Prohaska, cond. Bach Guild BG 555 (with Cantata No. 50).

——Marta Schilling (s); Gertrude Pitzinger (a); Heinz Marten (t); Gerhard Gröschel (bs); Rudolf Lamy Choral Society; Ansbach Bach Festival Orchestra, Ferdinand Leitner, cond. Decca dl 9557.

——Maria Stader (s); Elsa Cavelti (a); Ernst Haefliger (t); Hermann Schey (bs); Winterthur Mixed Chorus and City Orchestra, Walter Reinhart, cond. Concert Hall chc 60.

——Antonia Fahberg (s); Margarethe Bence (a); Helmut Krebs (t); Peter Roth-Ehrang (bs); Philippe Caillard Chorus; Pro Arte Chamber Orchestra (Munich), Kurt Redel, cond. Westminster xwn 18465.

THE PASSIONS AND ORATORIOS

St. Matthew Passion

The ideal performance of this tremendous masterwork has not yet been engraved on disks, if it has taken place at all. But one of the six available versions is about as good as we're likely to get—so good, indeed, that we have no hesitation in recommending it. That one is Scherchen's on Westminster. It takes four disks to Vox's three; one may not agree with every detail of interpretation or approve of every tempo; a soloist may not be far enough forward (as in No. 36); and the surfaces are far from noiseless. But this is a performance that results from profound insight and enkindling imagination. Each scene of the great drama is given its full value, and so is the pathos of the commentative and deliberative portions. The crowd's shout of *"Barrabam!"* comes like a thunderclap, while nothing could be more gentle and tender than the hushed pity of the onlookers in No. 25. Only in the stupendous final chorus does one get a feeling of excessive length, because of the slow tempo chosen. Cuenod is a first-class Evangelist, and Rehfuss sings the role of Jesus with sublime sweetness. The other soloists are not quite up to this standard but none of them is less than acceptable, and Standen is somewhat better than that. Rössl-Majdan has been in better form on other occasions, but her recitative and aria Nos. 60 and 61 are beautifully done.

Thomas's performance is less poetic and imaginative, but worthy of respect nevertheless. There are no frills or mannerisms. Thomas does especially well with the great final chorus, where the bass line is unusually clean and sturdy. It sounds as though he added bassoons there, with excellent effect. The vocal soloists are pretty much all of the same grade: they understand what they are about, and they do much pleasing work, though none of them has the virtuosity required to execute all of his or her music equally well. The chorus is properly balanced most of the time and has a good tone, which is not often distorted by the engineers.

The Grossmann is a straightforward reading, very good in some movements, rather routine in others. The chorus in clearly reproduced as a rule (it sounds a little blurred on Side 5), though the altos are sometimes a bit weak. Except for Kreuzberger, none of the soloists is quite as good as his opposite number on Westminster. The surfaces here are somewhat smoother than in that set.

Egmond conveys much of the drama of the Passion, and his tempos seem right. The soprano and alto soloists, however, are second-rate, and in the numbers for double chorus the sound is not as clear as it could be.

The Victor version, sung in English, is not complete. It omits three alto arias (Nos. 10, 61, 70), two bass arias (Nos. 51, 75), a tenor aria (No. 41), two chorales (Nos. 23, 55), a recitative (No. 50), and a recitative and chorus (No. 76). The chorus is well balanced, but the performance as a whole is rather stodgy and has little distinction except in the final chorus, which is nicely done.

The Columbia set was recorded from an actual performance at Amsterdam in 1939. Those who like to get the feeling of a concert hall will find here the usual coughing and the strange roar made by a large chorus rising to its feet. This album, too, is incomplete. A number of movements are omitted and some others are cut. Despite its age, the recording is not inadequate. But even if it were up-to-date, one could not recommend this version, in spite of some fine moments here and there. For this is an example of the nineteenth-century romantic approach to Bach. The tempos are often excessively slow, and there is a retard before practically every resting point—small retards on inner cadences, big ones at the ends of movements. In addition the music is distorted by romantic accents and swellings. Almost every suspension receives an extra stress *and* a retard.

——Magda Laszlo (s); Hilde Rössl-Majdan (a); Hugues Cuenod (t); Petre Munteanu (t); Heinz Rehfuss (bs); Richard Standen (bs); Symphony Orchestra and Chorus, Hermann Scherchen, cond. Four 12-in. WESTMINSTER WAL 401.

——Agnes Giebel (s); Lore Fischer (a); Helmut Kretschmar (t); Horst Günter (bs); Kantorei der Dreikönigskirche, Frankfurt; Collegium Musicum Orchestra, Kurt Thomas, cond. Four 12-in. OISEAU-LYRE OL 50113/16.

——Laurence Dutoit (s); Maria Nussbaumer (a); Rudolf Kreuzberger (t); Erich Majkut (t); Otto Wiener (bs); Harald Buchsbaum (bs); Akademie Kammerchor; Vienna Chamber Orchestra, Ferdinand Grossmann, cond. Three 12-in. VOX PL 8283.

——Corry Bijster (s); Annie Delorie (a); Willy van Hese (t); Carel Willink (bs); Amsterdam Oratorio Chorus; Vredescholen Boys' Choir; Rotterdam Chamber Orchestra, Piet van Egmond, cond. Three 12-in. CONCERT HALL CHS 1255.

——Lois Marshall (s); Margaret Stilwell (a); Edward Johnson (t); James Lamond (t); Donald Brown (bs); Eric Tredwell (bs); Toronto Mendelssohn Choir; Toronto Symphony Orchestra, Sir Ernest MacMillan, cond. Three 12-in. RCA VICTOR LBC 6101.

——Jo Vincent (s); Ilona Durigo (a); Louis van Tulder (t); Karl Erb (t); Hermann Schey (bs); William Ravelli (bs); Amsterdam Toonkunstchor; Concertgebouw Orchestra, Willem Mengelberg, cond. Three 12-in. COLUMBIA SL 179.

ST. JOHN PASSION

To make a choice among these performances is not easy. Important and obvious differences may be stated at once. The Victor version is sung in English; the other three in German. Shaw and Grossmann stress the drama in the work; the contrast between the lyric, meditative portions and the choral outbursts is much sharper in their performances than in the Ramin and Thomas, where the emphasis seems to be on purely musical values, on smooth, clean, well-sounding results. In the recitatives, Ramin, Thomas, and Grossmann use a harpsichord for the continuo when the Evangelist sings, an organ when Jesus sings; Shaw employs an organ throughout.

Ramin's approach is most effective in the lyric portions; a little more passion and incisiveness in the passages allotted to the crowd would have brought out better the bitterness of those sections. The tone of his chorus is pure and clean; it is well balanced except in the opening chorus and the *Ruht wohl*, where the tenors are a bit weak. The soloists are all excellent, although I would prefer a somewhat weightier tone for the soprano and alto. Even so, Höffgen's singing of *Es ist vollbracht* is especially moving, and she is aided by Alwin Bauer's exquisite playing of the gamba obbligato. Häfliger, the Evangelist, sings his taxing role with flexibility and intelligence, and does not lapse into falsetto for the high tones. The first-class recording maintains clarity even in the most contrapuntal tutti sections. The German text and an English translation are provided.

Thomas's chorus has a round and pleasing sound, if not the utmost clarity in contrapuntal sections. Herbert Hess, the Evangelist, negotiates the high notes smoothly but, in keeping with the rather restrained quality of this whole performance, maintains the same, somewhat detached mood in all the varying events he narrates. Paul Gümmer, in the role of Jesus, sings sweetly and with excellent intonation. Gunthild Weber and Sibylla Plate perform their arias acceptably; the latter is the only alto of the four who has a real trill. The performance as a whole has a good deal of warmth and fervor, but lacks the power and violence occasionally required. The recording is on a relatively low dynamic level, and the last three sides contain some surface noise and crackles. No text is supplied.

In clarity and flexibility of line and beauty of tone, Shaw's chorus is, as usual, superior to its competitors. It is free of the soprano domination found in so many recorded choral groups; even in the four-part chorales, where the melody is in the top voice, Bach's wonderful inner parts come fully alive. If, in this performance, two or three of the chorales have a weightiness that does not seem to be called for in the context or by the words, the other choral sections are very well done. The forcefulness of the dramatic portions never becomes theatrical, and such a movement as *Mein teurer Heiland*, for bass solo and chorus, is performed with an ecstatic tenderness unequaled in the other versions. Blake Stern, as the Evangelist, sings with more color and variety than Hess. Harrell (Jesus), Slick (Pilate), and Matthen (arias) are all satisfactory. Adele Addison's voice is rather small but pleasing, and Blanche Thebom sings her arias acceptably, though in *Von den Strikken* (No. 11) her phrases are not always clearly articulated. At times, as in the aria just mentioned and in *Ich folge dir* No. 13), one hears only the naked bass, the right-hand part of the continuo being either not played at all or played inaudibly. Only the English translation used here is provided.

Grossmann, like Shaw, brings out the intensity and drama of this Passion. He is aided by competent soloists. His soprano is in fact perhaps the best of the four. Unfortunately, however, the tone of the chorus, while well balanced, is somewhat rougher and cruder than that of the other three, and some of the chorales are done with a heavy hand. In the exquisite bass arioso, *Betrachte, meine Seel'* (No. 31), which is beautifully performed in the other versions and especially by Shaw, the instruments are too loud for the voice. Throughout the work the bass instruments are more prominent than they need be; where they double the choral basses, one can scarcely hear those voices. This has the noisiest surfaces of the four recordings.

——Agnes Giebel (s); Marga Höffgen (a); Ernst Häfliger (t); Franz Kelch (bs; Jesus); Hans-Olaf Hudemann (bs; Petrus, Pilatus); Thomanerchor and Gewandhausorchester (Leipzig), Günther Ramin, cond. Three 12-in. ARCHIVE ARC 3045/47.
——Adele Addison (s); Blanche Thebom (a); Blake

Stern (t); Leslie Chabay (t); Mack Harrell (bar); Paul Matthen (bs); Daniel Slick (bs); Robert Shaw Chorale, Collegiate Chorale; RCA Victor Orchestra, Robert Shaw, cond. Three 12-in. RCA VICTOR LM 6103.

——Gisela Rathauscher (s); Elfriede Hofstätter (a); Ferry Gruber (t); Rudolf Kreuzberger (t); Walter Berry (bs); Akademie Kammerchor; Vienna Symphony Orchestra, Ferdinand Grossmann, cond. Three 12-in. VOX PL 6550.

——Gunthild Weber (s); Sibylla Plate (a); Herbert Hess (t); Paul Gümmer (bs); Kantorei der Dreikönigskirche (Frankfurt); Collegium Musicum Orchestra, Kurt Thomas, cond. Three 12-in. OISEAU-LYRE OL 50023/25.

ST. JOHN PASSION—ABRIDGED VERSION

This performance is neither unmusical nor insensitive, and those who would be satisfied with only some of the important portions of the Passion on a single disk may find this one acceptable. A harpsichord is the continuo instrument here. The numbers that are retained are given complete, except for the recitative, which is often considerably abbreviated, and for the great first and last (*Ruht wohl*) choruses, which are cut before the repeat. The highs are very much exaggerated; I had to turn the treble control way down to achieve tone approaching reality.

——Berta Seidl (s); Hilde Rössl-Majdan (a); Erich Majkut (t); Otto Wiener (bs); Walter Berry (bs); Austrian Symphony Orchestra and Chorus, Gottfried Preinfalk, cond. REMINGTON R 199-78.

CHRISTMAS ORATORIO

First performed at Leipzig in 1734, the *Christmas Oratorio* contains a number of movements adapted from earlier secular cantatas and other works, as well as some new material. It is in six sections and was designed to be performed one section at a time on six days from Christmas to Epiphany. Because of this, and because of the predominantly lyric—rather than dramatic—character of the work, it is not advisable to play the whole cycle at one sitting. If the sections are set off from one another, the many splendid choruses and lovely arias will have a better chance to achieve their full effect.

The Archive recording seems clearly the best of the three available to the writer. Its soloists are all satisfactory; its chorus has an attractive tone, is well balanced, and sings with vitality, and excellent work is done by the first trumpet and the solo violin.

Neither of the other two versions is particularly distinguished. Miss Weber's singing for Oiseau-Lyre is not quite as sturdy as for Archive, and the other soloists do not maintain the level of their best moments as consistently as do those in the Archive. No text is supplied by Oiseau-Lyre, and on the review set there are defective grooves in No. 3 of Part I.

——Gunthild Weber (s); Sieglinde Wagner (a); Helmut Krebs (t); Heinz Rehfuss (bs); Berliner Motettenchor; RIAS Kammerchor; Berlin Philharmonic Orchestra, Fritz Lehmann (Parts I-IV), Günther Arndt (Parts V-VI), conds. Three 12-in. Archive ARC 3079/81.

——Elisabeth Roon (s); Dagmar Herrmann (a);

Erich Majkut (t); Walter Berry (bs); Akademie
Kammerchor, Vienna Symphony Orchestra, Ferdi-
nand Grossmann, cond. Three 12-in. Vox PL 7713.
——Gunthild Weber (s); Lore Fischer (a); Heinz
Marten (t); Horst Gunther (bs); Orchestra and
Choir of the Detmold Academy of Music and the
Collegium Pro Arte, Kurt Thomas, cond. Three
12-in. OISEAU-LYRE OL 50001/3.
[——M. Schilling (s); R. Michaelis (a); W. Hoh-
mann (t); B. Müller (bs); Stuttgart Chorus and
Swabian Symphony, Hans Grischkat, cond. Four
12-in. REMINGTON 199-118.]

EASTER ORATORIO

The music of this work is basically the same as
that of a secular cantata, *Entfliehet, verschwindet,*
composed in 1725 and whose rediscovery was announced in 1942. About 1736 Bach adjusted this
music to a rhymed German text suitable for Easter.
The result is rather like a long cantata, without
the chorales and with the chorus active only near
the beginning (after two introductory instrumental
movements) and at the end. In between are recitatives and arias. The expressive second movement, a
fine tenor aria, and the triumphant final chorus
are high points in a work that is not very impressive
as a whole. Prohaska's tempos are a bit livelier than
Grossmann's and seem better suited to the text.
The voices of his soprano and alto soloists have a
warmer quality; the two basses are about equally
satisfactory; and Grossmann's tenor, it seems to me,
has a slight advantage. There is a little distortion
in the last movement of the Bach Guild disk, but
its surfaces are quieter.

——Maja Weis-Osborn (s); Hilde Rössl-Majdan
(a); Kurt Equiluz (t); Walter Berry (bs); Akademiechor; Vienna Chamber Orchestra, Felix Prohaska, cond. BACH GUILD BG 507.

——Laurence Dutoit (s); Maria Nussbaumer (a);
Franz Gruber (t); Otto Wiener (bs); Akademie
Kammerchor; Pro Musica Chamber Orchestra,
Ferdinand Grossmann, cond. VOX PL 8620.

ARIAS, DUETS, ETC.

GEISTLICHE LIEDER

The *Geistliche Lieder* comprise the sixty-nine
sacred songs published by Schemelli plus six songs
from the notebook for Anna Magdalena Bach.
They are all for a solo voice with continuo (here
harpsichord and cello). Varying opinions are held
concerning which of the songs in the Schemelli collection are by Bach. The consensus is that the
majority are not, but he seems to have had a hand
in supplying or improving the figured bass for these.
In any case, there are many lovely pieces here, along
with a number that are not outstanding. They are
all nicely sung, but the general sameness of texture
and similarity of mood make this collection valu-
able chiefly for occasional sampling and for reference
purposes. Westminster supplies the score for all the
music.

——Hilde Rössl-Majdan (a); Hugues Cuenod (t);
Richard Harand, cello; Franz Holetschek, harpsi-

chord. Four 12-in. WESTMINSTER XWN 4405 or 18386/89.

MISCELLANEOUS COLLECTIONS

Only one of the twelve pieces on the two disks made by the Bach Aria Group (*Ich esse mit Freuden,* from Cantata No. 84) is available elsewhere on LP. These are all well chosen, nicely varied in mood, and, on the whole, very competently performed. The soprano, alto, and bass sing satisfactorily; the tenor (who has two arias), less so. There is especially good playing by the flute (Julius Baker) and first violin (Maurice Wilk). A piano is used for the continuo throughout, and ordinary cello instead of a violoncello piccolo in *Mein gläubiges Herze,* and an ordinary oboe instead of an oboe d'amore in *Wenn des Kreuzes Bitterkeiten.* The recording is acceptable, although the bass seems a little distant in two of his arias and the alto in one of hers and the surfaces are not as quiet as they could be.

——"Six Sacred Arias by J. S. Bach" (*Süsser trost,* from Cantata No. 151; *Menschen glaubt,* from Cantata No. 7; *Nichts ist es spät und frühe,* from Cantata No. 97; *Ich esse mit Freuden,* from Cantata No. 84; *Wie furchtsam wanken meine Schritte,* from Cantata No. 33; *Handle nicht nach deine Rechten,* from Cantata No. 101). Jean Carlton (s); Margaret Tobias (a); Robert Harmon (t); Norman Farrow (bs); Bach Aria Group, William H. Scheide, cond. 10-in. M-G-M E 89.

——"Arias and Duets from Church Cantatas" (*Mein gläubiges Herze,* from Cantata No. 68; *Es ist vollbracht,* from Cantata No. 159; *Jesus nimmt die Sünder an,* from Cantata No. 113; *Ja, ja, ich halte Jesum feste,* from Cantata No. 157; *Sei bemüht in dieser Zeit,* from Cantata No. 185; *Wenn des Kreuzes Bitterkeiten,* from Cantata No. 99). Performers same as above. 10-in. M-G-M E 115.

The eight selections on the Bach Guild disk are equally divided between Rössl-Majdan and Cuenod. All of them come from the complete recordings discussed in their proper places above. Both singers are represented here at their very considerable best. Highly recommended to those who want a sampling of fine sacred arias.

——"Great Arias from the Cantatas" (*Saget mir geschwinde,* from the Easter Oratorio; *O sel'ger Tag!,* from Cantata No. 63; *Getrost es fast,* from Cantata No. 133; *Komm, du süsse Todesstunde,* from Cantata No. 161; *Bäche von gesalznen Zähren,* from Cantata No. 21; *So klage du,* from Cantata No. 46; *Erfreue dich,* from Cantata No. 21; *Verbirgt mein Hirte,* from Cantata No. 104). Hilde Rössl-Majdan (a); Hugues Cuenod (t); orchestras cond. by Michael Gielen, Felix Prohaska, Jonathan Sternberg. BACH GUILD BG 526.

Of the seven arias in the Victor set, two are for soprano, one each for alto, tenor, and bass, one is a duet for soprano and bass, and the last a duet for soprano and tenor. Only one of these items is available elsewhere on LP (the duet *Gott, ach Gott,* in the recording of the complete cantata), and it is sung better here. The soloists are all competent, and there is some excellent instrumental playing. A piano is used for the continuo throughout and flutes instead of recorders are employed in *Die Seele ruht*. These arias seem to have been recorded at a lower level than the complete cantatas in the same set.

——"Bach Cantatas and Arias" (*Die Seele ruht*, from Cantata No. 127; *Mein Gott, wie lang*, from Cantata No. 155; *Erschütt're dich nur nicht*, from Cantata No. 99; *Jesu, beuge doch mein Herze*, from Cantata No. 47; *Gott, ach Gott*, from Cantata No. 79; *Christi Glieder*, from Cantata No. 132; *Ehre sei Gott in der Höhe*, from Cantata No. 110). Eileen Farrell (s); Carol Smith (a); Jan Peerce (t); Norman Farrow (bs); Orchestra and Bach Aria Group Chorus, Frank Brieff, cond. Two 12-in. RCA VICTOR LM 6023 (with Cantatas Nos. 60, 41, and 42).

Warm singing by Carol Brice is offered on one of the Columbia disks. Long phrases float effortlessly, and there are only one or two tiny spots that indicate that this artist's technique could be further improved. There are puzzling little cuts in the arias from the Mass—the instrumental postlude of the Agnus Dei and a ritornel of the *Qui sedes*. These are surprising because each one only amounts to a few measures and because there is, on the other hand, an uncalled-for repetition of the last section of the *Et exsultavit*. Richer, more vibrant singing, by Kathleen Ferrier, is found on the London record. This has a more resonant sound than the Columbia. It is not, however, recommended as a Ferrier "Bach recital," because all four of the arias, wonderful as they are, are in pretty much the same mood. But to play one or two of them at a time is a stirring experience, if you don't mind the English texts in the excerpts from the Passions. The review copy was rather crackly.

——"Sacred Arias of J. S. Bach" (Agnus Dei and *Qui sedes,* from Mass in B minor; *Esurientes implevit bonis* and *Et exsultavit,* from the Magnificat). Carol Brice (a); Columbia Broadcasting Concert Orchestra, Daniel Saidenburg, cond. Co-LUMBIA ML 4108 (with Mahler: *Songs of a Wayfarer*).

——"Bach and Handel Arias" (*Qui sedes* and Agnus Dei, from Mass in B minor; *Grief for Sin,* from *St. Matthew Passion; All is Fulfilled,* from *St. John Passion*). Kathleen Ferrier (a); London Philharmonic Orchestra, Sir Adrian Boult, cond. 12-in. LONDON LL 688 (with four Handel arias).

Schwarzkopf presents two little gems on her Columbia record. Here we have beautifully sustained singing in *Schafe können sicher weiden* (from Cantata No. 208) and an elegant performance of the lively *Mein gläubiges Herze* (from Cantata No. 68). Flutes are used instead of recorders in the first, and an ordinary cello instead of a violoncello piccolo in the other.

——Elisabeth Schwarzkopf (s); instrumental ensemble, Peter Gellhorn, cond. COLUMBIA ML 4792 (with Cantatas Nos. 51 and 82).

KEYBOARD WORKS

Because of the special nature of the instrument, any attempt to evaluate recordings of performances on the organ must be even more than usually subjective. Generally speaking, any good piano sounds pretty much like any other; and any normal orchestra playing a specific work will be constituted like any other playing that work, give or take a few strings. But not only are there radical differences in sound between the great families of organs—for example, between "baroque" and "symphonic" instruments—there also are important differences between instruments of the same family, since no organ is built exactly like another. In addition, each performer usually has his own ideas about registration; even if two players used the same instrument, the results would probably differ in color. In the following discussion of Bach's organ works, where two or more equally acceptable performances of a work are available (which happens not seldom), I have given preference to the one that sounds most pleasing to my own ears, though I am well aware that other listeners might choose differently and with as much justice.

Another complication in judging organ records

involves not the quality but the kind of recording. The quality of organ recordings has improved enormously in recent years, and it is astonishing, in view of the tremendous acoustical problems, how often the reproduction is absolutely first-class. But one must choose between two points of view. One is that the recording should be "realistic," reproducing faithfully the sound of an organ in a church or cathedral—echoes, reverberations, and all. Not only is this supposed to give the hearer the feeling of "reality," but it is thought to represent the composer's intentions most faithfully. After all, the theory is, Bach knew a great deal about church acoustics and certainly would have taken them into account when composing. And so we have some recordings in which the sounds, after leaving the pipes, dance around merrily, looping through the vast upper spaces and mingling gaily with their newly arriving brothers so that it is hard to tell which is which. As a practicing musician, Bach surely did know a great deal about church acoustics and he made some provision for them, but not, I think, much. Otherwise he would have written only slow chordal pieces with plenty of rests. Most of his organ works show, in their constantly moving parts, in the importance and fine detail of the inner voices, that he must have had in mind a kind of ideal enclosure in which the sound, while live and resonant, would be sharp and clear, never blurring rapid movement or obscuring contrapuntal texture. It is to this kind of recording—and fortunately there is a good deal of it—that my vote has gone when there was a choice.

In recordings of works for stringed keyboard instruments, preference has been given, other things being more or less equal, to performances on the harpsichord. Bach probably intended some of these works for clavichord, but no doubt he expected that even those would be played occasionally on the harpsichord. There is, moreover, only one LP on which a clavichord is used (*see* the Two-Part Inventions, S. 772-786). Performances of Bach on the piano pose a special problem. The harpsichord with stops and coupling mechanism is capable of color variety of a type impossible to achieve on a piano. The pianist, deprived of such possibilities, tries to avoid monotony in other ways, often relying on the color properties peculiar to the piano. Actually many pianistic effects were born of the romantic school of piano composition and are inseparably associated with it in our minds. As a result the ordinary pianist's innocent attempts to beguile the listener while playing music not intended for his instrument often succeed only in evoking a feeling remote from Bach's. Rare are the pianists who somehow manage to keep interest alive without doing violence to Bach's style.

ORGAN WORKS

Before we discuss individual works, some general comments on a few collections may be found useful. The largest of these is the Archive series of eighteen disks, which present Helmut Walcha playing on the Arp Schnitger organ now in Cappel and on the smaller of the two organs at St. Jakobi in Lübeck. Both instruments seem to be ideal for Bach, and the recording is superb. (Some of these performances, with less quiet surfaces, previously had been issued in this country under the Decca label.) Equally fine are the organ—in the Church of Our Lady at Skänninge, Sweden—and the recording in Carl Weinrich's series for Westminster, of which six "volumes" are available as this is written.

In another class are two albums by Dr. Albert Schweitzer. As the recordings of E. Power Biggs show, Columbia engineers have successfully captured the sound of many different organs; one must conclude, therefore, that some peculiarity of Dr. Schweitzer's instrument, in the parish church of his home town of Gunsbach in Alsace, militates against best results in recording. Nevertheless, the sound in the second album (SL 223) is less dim and distant than in the first (SL 175); and in any case one may value the two sets for reasons other than mere beauty of sound. Despite the tonal shortcomings of the organ and despite occasional evidence that Dr. Schweitzer's technique is no longer what it once must have been, these albums together with their elaborate notes remain affecting mementoes of the great humanitarian's lifelong reverence for his favorite composer.

SONATAS (6), S. 525-530

Composed at Leipzig in the 1720s. These sonatas, says Schweitzer, are "the *Gradus ad Parnassum* for every organist. Whoever has studied them thoroughly will encounter no further difficulties in either old or modern organ-literature, having already met and conquered them all in these Sonatas." But they are, of course, far more than mere exercises for hands and feet. While they may not have the emotional power of the chorale preludes and the greatest of the preludes and fugues, their variety and superb construction make them very good listening indeed. Walcha keeps the voices sharply differentiated and the texture transparent; and the moments when the pedal is a little weak and behind time are not enough to mar the set. Germani plays well, too, but occasionally, as in the first two movements of No. 2 or the last of No. 4, the middle voice is not clear enough. The pedal of his instrument, not identified in the review set, sometimes emits indistinct rumbles. The organ at the Church of Saint-Merry in Paris, which is used by Mme. Alain, has sounded better on other disks. Here, some of the pedal stops are weak and have little character; they apparently do not "speak" readily and sometimes lag behind the manuals. At the other end of the tonal spectrum Mme. Alain seems to be fond of stops that sound rather shrill; and the middle voice is sometimes too faint.

A similar difficulty obtains with the organ employed by Eggington, that of the Meaux Cathedral, whose pedal produces vague noises, among which definite pitches can be discerned only occasionally. The two sonatas recorded by Biggs, in Boston's Symphony Hall, are very well done and recommended to anyone who wants only two of the six works. Hilliar chooses intriguing colors for the fast movements and indulges in a mild use of dotted rhythms in the Finale of his sonata.

——Helmut Walcha. ARCHIVE ARC 3013/4. Two 12-in.

——Fernando Germani. RCA VICTOR LHMV 601. Two 12-in.

——Marie-Claire Alain. HAYDN SOCIETY HSL 119/20 (with S. 562, 572, 590). Two 12-in.

——(S. 525-528 only) John Eggington. OISEAU-LYRE OL 50123.

——(S. 525, 526 only) E. Power Biggs. COLUMBIA ML 4285 (with S. 541, 544).

——(S. 525 only) George Faxon. AEOLIAN-SKINNER "The King of Instruments" Vol. II (with S. 593 1st movement, 646, 648, 650 and works by Davies, Alain, Langlais, Sowerby).

——(S. 528 only) Edgar Hilliar. AEOLIAN-SKINNER "The King of Instruments" Vol. IV (with a chorale prelude and works by Pachelbel, Loiellet, Couperin, Dupré, Arne).

PRELUDE AND FUGUE IN C, S. 531

Weimar, about 1709, or possibly earlier at Lüneburg. There is more majesty in Schweitzer's Prelude than in any of the others, even though the sounds of his instrument are occasionally blurred. Walcha takes the Prelude much more quickly and it consequently loses its pomp. The Fugue is a light footed, graceful work under his hands. With Heiller, the Prelude, though taken at about the same tempo as Schweitzer's, sounds growly; and the Fugue, while well played, is not as transparent in texture as with Walcha. Weinrich's performance for Westminster is rather metronomic and favors a registration that sounds unpleasantly piercing to me. The sound of his M-G-M recording, on the other hand, is a little distant and by no means precise as to pitch. There is, consequently, no all-round first-class recording of this work.

——Walcha. ARCHIVE ARC 3015 (with S. 532, 533, 535, 537).

——Anton Heiller. EPIC LC 3261 (with S. 582, 768).

——Carl Weinrich. WESTMINSTER XWN 18499 (with S. 536, 539, 541, 543).

——Weinrich. M-G-M E 3015 (with S. 536, 543, and transcriptions by Segovia).

——(Prelude only) Albert Schweitzer. COLUMBIA SL 175 (with S. 532, 542, 543, 564, 588, 6 chorale preludes, and Mendelssohn: Sonata No. 6). Three 12-in.

PRELUDE AND FUGUE IN D, S. 532

Weimar, about 1709 or possibly earlier in Arnstadt. An elaborate work, whose Prelude has the slow-fast-slow shape of the French overture and whose Fugue is a long working-out of a jolly theme that begins by chasing its tail. From the musical standpoint, Mme. Alain does as good a job as any, displaying a nice sense of color, which makes itself felt despite some surface noise and the shrillness of some of her stops. Walcha is a little less interesting but better recorded. Heiller's Prelude is darker in color and not as clear in texture as Walcha's or Alain's. There is nothing particularly distinguished about any of the other versions. Fox's performance is that of a virtuoso, but the wrong sort: he changes registration frequently but his colors are seldom subtle, and for some reason he blasts out the Adagio at the end of the Prelude in violent contrast to what has gone before.

——Alain. HAYDN SOCIETY HSL 148 (with S. 541, 544, 545, 548).

——Walcha. ARCHIVE ARC 3015 (*see* S. 531).

——Heiller. EPIC LC 3132 (with S. 543, 565, 566, 589).

——Weinrich. WESTMINSTER XWN 18427 (with S. 533, 534, 544).

——Marilyn Mason. AEOLIAN-SKINNER "The King of Instruments" Vol. VII (with works by Walther, Kerll, Pachelbel, Crandell, Copland, Wright).

——Phillip Steinhaus, BOSTON B 700 (with S. 564; Reger: Variations and Fugue on an Original Theme, Op. 73).

——Jeanne Demessieux. LONDON LL 319 (with S. 565; Franck: Pastorale; Fantaisie in A).

——Virgil Fox. RCA VICTOR LM 1963 (with S. 565, 577, chorale preludes, etc).

——(Prelude only) Schweitzer. COLUMBIA SL 175 (*see* S. 531).

——(Fugue only) Eggington. OISEAU-LYRE OL 50012 (with S. 541, 548, 564, 649).

PRELUDE AND FUGUE IN E MINOR, S. 533

Weimar, about 1709 or perhaps earlier in Arnstadt. Sometimes known as the "little E minor," this short work has power and pathos: Walcha begins the Prelude rather fast but then slows down, a treatment that seems to suit the improvisatory character of the opening section. Schweitzer and Cochereau take the whole work very slowly. The sound of the latter's instrument (the organ at Nôtre-Dame in Paris) is poorly recorded. As played by both Weinrich and Nowakowski, the Prelude sounds metronomic. In Coke-Jephcott's solemn performance of the Fugue and Nowakowski's rather matter-of-fact one the voices are not always clearly distinguishable. (The Schmieder numbers on the 10-inch Telefunken disk are confused; on the 12-inch, this work is wrongly labeled S. 548.) Commette's version is marred by excessive reverberation.

——Walcha. ARCHIVE ARC 3015 (*see* S. 531).

——Schweitzer. COLUMBIA 5SL 223 (with S. 534, 536, 538, 541, 543, 544, 546, 547, 565, 582, 6 chorale preludes). Three 12-in.

——Weinrich. WESTMINSTER XWN 18427 (*see* S. 532).

——Norman Coke-Jephcott. AEOLIAN-SKINNER "The King of Instruments" Vol. VIII (with 2 chorale preludes and works by Purcell, Vierne, Coke-Jephcott).

——Anton Nowakowski. TELEFUNKEN LGM 65030 (with S. 572, 582). 10-in. Or LGX 66059 (with S. 544, 545, 565, 572, 582).

——Pierre Cochereau. OISEAU-LYRE OL 50152 (with S. 544, 547).

——Edouard Commette. ANGEL 35368 (with S. 542, 543, 546, 562, 565, 2 chorale preludes).

PRELUDE AND FUGUE IN F MINOR, S. 534

Weimar, about 1716. All three performances of this rather uneven work have their merits and defects. Schweitzer's is perhaps the most eloquent, even though it drags in spots and even though there are moments when either the player's fingers or the instrument's pipes do not respond efficiently. His registration during much of the Fugue is somber, no doubt in accordance with his view of the music as expressing suffering. Walcha and Weinrich take a somewhat brighter view; no one, however, can do much about making the dull spots in the Fugue meaningful. Weinrich's Prelude is just a shade faster than Walcha's and by that much the more matter-of-fact.

——Schweitzer. COLUMBIA 5SL 223 (*see* S. 533).

——Walcha. ARCHIVE ARC 3020 (with S. 564, 566, 572).

——Weinrich. WESTMINSTER XWN 18427 (*see* S. 532).

PRELUDE AND FUGUE IN G MINOR, S. 535

Weimar, about 1709, or perhaps earlier in Arnstadt. Surprisingly, there is only one recording of this fine early work. Walcha plays the improvisatory Prelude sensitively and renders bright and clear the interestingly worked-out Fugue.

——Walcha. ARCHIVE ARC 3015 (*see* S. 531).

PRELUDE AND FUGUE IN A, S. 536

Weimar, about 1716. Schweitzer's Prelude seems too slow, but the pace at which he takes the unusually lyric Fugue gives it the calm serenity that he believes Bach wished to express. The others all play both the Prelude and the Fugue more quickly. The result is a gentle swing that brings the Prelude to life, and some loss of tranquility but none of gladness of spirit in the Fugue. The sound of Litaize's instrument is a little blurred, but he performs the Fugue tenderly. The choice, it seems to me, lies among Weinrich, Walcha, and Viderø, and since there is not much difference in the interpretation,

the determining element may be registration and
quality of instrument. The unidentified organ used
by Weinrich on M-G-M sounds rather harsh compared to the other three instruments in question,
and to me the colors employed by Walcha and
Weinrich on Westminster are the loveliest.

——Walcha. ARCHIVE ARC 3016 (with S. 538-540).

——Weinrich. WESTMINSTER XWN 18499 (*see* S.
531).

——Finn Viderø. HAYDN SOCIETY HSL 128 (with S.
544, 572, 590).

——Weinrich. M-G-M E 3015 (*see* S. 531).

——Schweitzer. COLUMBIA 5SL 223 (*see* S. 533).

——Gaston Litaize. LONDON DTL 93037 (with S.
552, 565, 582).

PRELUDE (FANTASY) AND FUGUE IN C MINOR, S. 537

Weimar, about 1716. Both artists do well with the
brooding, contemplative Prelude but neither succeeds in making the Fugue sound shorter than it is.
Marchal's instrument, the organ at Saint-Eustache
in Paris, is recorded somewhat dimly, and details of
the counterpoint are obscured.

——Walcha. ARCHIVE ARC 3015 (*see* S. 531).

——André Marchal. LONDON DTL 93056 (with S.
542, 544, 546).

PRELUDE (TOCCATA) AND FUGUE ("DORIAN"), S.
538

Leipzig, between 1727 and 1736, if not earlier in
Cöthen (the Fugue may have been written about
1716 in Weimar). The majestic grandeur of this
monumental work is well conveyed by the first three
organists. Schweitzer's Prelude again seems over-

deliberate. It's a tossup between Weinrich and Walcha, with my vote going to the former on the basis of his registration. Heiller and Dupré are not much better than routine here; and the latter's pedal sounds muffled.

——Weinrich. WESTMINSTER WN 18148 (with S. 566, 588, 589).

——Walcha. ARCHIVE ARC 3016 (see S. 536).

——Schweitzer. COLUMBIA 5SL 223 (see S. 533).

——Heiller. EPIC LC 3367 (with S. 540, 562, 569).

——Marcel Dupré. OVERTONE 13 (with S. 540 and chorale preludes).

——(Toccata only) Alec Wyton. AEOLIAN-SKINNER "The King of Instruments" Vol. VI (with works by Sweelinck, Stanley, Sowerby, Whitlock, Britten, Howells).

PRELUDE AND FUGUE IN D MINOR, S. 539

Leipzig, 1724 or 1725. The grave Prelude is beautifully played by Weinrich and the Fugue, which is based on the Fugue in the G minor Sonata for unaccompanied violin, is neatly done by both artists.

——Weinrich. WESTMINSTER XWN 18499 (see S. 531).

——(Fugue only) Walcha. ARCHIVE ARC 3016 (see S. 536).

PRELUDE (TOCCATA) AND FUGUE IN F, S. 540

The Fugue: Weimar, about 1716; the Toccata: apparently later, in Cöthen. Another one of the giant masterworks. The Toccata begins with a pedalpoint that lasts for fifty-four measures, and soon afterward there is another one virtually as long.

The tensions that build up over these sustained tones are more effectively conveyed by Walcha and Weinrich than by Biggs, whose tempo is a little faster than theirs and whose pedal tones are a little softer. As between the first two, there is little to choose. Both the Archive and the regular Westminster disk are very well recorded, but the LAB version of the same performance by Weinrich is even clearer and brighter. My own choice here, however, is Walcha, mainly because his Fugue is less deliberate than Weinrich's. Heiller's performance of the Toccata is acceptable but in the Fugue the lines are blurred. The Dupré version is rather mild.

——Walcha. ARCHIVE ARC 3016 (*see* S. 536).

——Weinrich. WESTMINSTER W-LAB 7023 (with S. 565, 635, 679). Or XWN 18260 (with S. 564, 565, 582).

——Heiller. EPIC LC 3367 (*see* S. 538).

——Dupré. OVERTONE 13 (*see* S. 538).

——(Toccata only) Biggs. COLUMBIA ML 4097 (with S. 542, 552, 680).

PRELUDE AND FUGUE IN G, S. 541

Leipzig, 1724 or 1725. "Over this Prelude and Fugue," wrote Widor and Schweitzer in their edition of it, "something like a sunny sky seems to be spread. They are eloquent with a great, serene confidence that banishes care from troubled hearts." The most vital readings are those by Biggs, Alain, and Walcha; but Walcha's Fugue is rather pedestrian and Alain's pedal sometimes lags slightly behind, which leaves Biggs. Weinrich does not sound inspired by anything in this work. Eggington suffers from too much reverberation. Prince-Joseph plays on a pedal harpsichord, which would have been more interesting if he had performed a work that Bach wrote for that instrument instead of one that is plainly indicated in Bach's manuscript as for organ.

——Biggs. COLUMBIA ML 4285 (*see* S. 525).

——Walcha. ARCHIVE ARC 3017 (with S. 542, 543, 562).

——Alain. HAYDN SOCIETY HSL 148 (*see* S. 532).

——Schweitzer. COLUMBIA 5SL 223 (*see* S. 533).

——Weinrich. WESTMINSTER XWN 18499 (*see* S. 531).

——Eggington. OISEAU-LYRE OL 50012 (*see* S. 532).

——(Prelude only) Bruce Prince-Joseph, harpsichord. COOK 11312 (with S. 593; choral works by various composers).

PRELUDE (FANTASY) AND FUGUE IN G MINOR, S. 542

Cöthen, about 1720. This is the "great" G minor Fantasy and Fugue, one of the most popular of the organ works. The most dramatic treatment of the Fantasy is Biggs's, but the speed with which he plays it renders some passages trivial, and he races through the Fugue. At the opposite pole, as regards tempo, is Schweitzer, who takes both movements broadly. His Fantasy is rather regular and his Fugue somewhat labored, but each builds up power and momentum. Unfortunately, the lines are often blurred in this recording. They are sometimes indistinct in the Marchal disk, too. The tone of that artist's instrument is not very attractive here, and there is a lack of spontaneity in the playing.

The Nunez disk, recorded on a Mexican organ said to be the largest in this hemisphere, is remarkable chiefly for its effect of cathedral spaciousness. The version that seems to me to sound best and wear best is Walcha's. Next I have put Richter's, similar in general type to Schweitzer's but more clearly recorded.

——Walcha. ARCHIVE ARC 3017 (*see* S. 541).

——Karl Richter. LONDON LL 1175 (with S. 548, 3 chorale preludes).

——Schweitzer. COLUMBIA SL 175 (*see* S. 531).

——Marchal. LONDON DTL 93056 (*see* S. 537).

——Biggs. COLUMBIA ML 4097 (*see* S. 540).

——Alfonso Vega Nunez. COOK 1056 (with S. 578, 593).

——(Fantasy only) Commette. ANGEL 35368 (*see* S. 533).

PRELUDE AND FUGUE IN A MINOR, S. 543

Prelude: Weimar, about 1709; Fugue: original version, for clavier, in Cöthen; revision, for organ, in Leipzig. A powerful and lively work, whose Prelude has passages of almost romantic intensity and whose Fugue proceeds with inexorable drive. These qualities are best brought out, it seems to me, by Heitmann and Weinrich on M-G-M. It is difficult to choose between them. Schweitzer's Prelude is expressive, but in his Fugue the inner voices do not come through clearly. Walcha, Heiller, Demessieux, and Weinrich on Westminster are all acceptable but not outstanding. The main point of interest in Coci's performance is that she plays, quite tastefully, on the giant organ at West Point.

——Fritz Heitmann. TELEFUNKEN LGX 66037 (with

S. 565 and works by various composers: "Organ Music from Sweelinck to Hindemith"). Two 12-in.

——Weinrich. M-G-M E 3015 (*see* S. 531).

——Schweitzer. COLUMBIA 5SL 223 (*see* S. 533).

——Walcha. ARCHIVE ARC 3017 (*see* S. 541).

——Weinrich. WESTMINSTER XWN 18499 (*see* S. 531).

——Heiller. EPIC LC 3132 (*see* S. 532).

——Demessieux. LONDON LL 946 (with S. 564, 577, 599, 626, 641).

——Claire Coci. VOX DL 210 (with S. 565, 582, 659).

——(Prelude only) Commette. ANGEL 35368 (*see* S. 533).

——(Fugue only) Schweitzer. COLUMBIA SL 175 (*see* S. 531).

PRELUDE AND FUGUE IN B MINOR, S. 544

Leipzig, between 1727 and 1736. One of the great masterworks, with a magnificent Prelude in which the melody shoots forth proliferations in all the voices, and a powerful Fugue. Several good performances here. For fire and authority in the Prelude, Schweitzer seems to take first place, but he does not help Bach in the middle part of the Fugue. There, where the composer marks time for a while, Schweitzer employs weak, dull stops. Viderø's Prelude also has more vitality than his Fugue but the over-all effect is fairly consistent. So is that of Walcha's performance, where interest is sustained in the middle portion of the Fugue by a nice choice of registration. Biggs's version is on a par with these. There is in fact no very important difference in quality among the first four performances listed below. The others have no special distinction, and in all of these except the Weinrich there are defects of one sort or another in the instrument or its recording.

——Viderø. HAYDN SOCIETY HSL 128 (*see* S. 536).

——Walcha. ARCHIVE ARC 3018 (with S. 545, 546, 550).

——Biggs. COLUMBIA ML 4285 (*see* S. 525).

——Schweitzer. COLUMBIA 5SL 223 (*see* S. 533).

——Weinrich. WESTMINSTER XWN 18427 (*see* S. 532).

——Alain. HAYDN SOCIETY 148 (*see* S. 532).

——Nowakowski. TELEFUNKEN LGX 66059 (*see* S. 533).

——Marchal. LONDON DTL 93056 (*see* S. 537).

——Cochereau. OISEAU-LYRE OL 50125 (*see* S. 533).

PRELUDE AND FUGUE IN C, S. 545

Prelude: Leipzig, about 1730; Fugue: earlier, toward the end of the Weimar period. White's small American organ, Nowakowski's Danish one, and Alain's French one sound coarse and unclear compared to the Schnitger played by Walcha.

——Walcha. ARCHIVE ARC 3018 (*see* S. 544).

——Ernest White. MOLLER "Music for the Organ" Vol. 2 (with works by Vierne, Reger, Widor, Dandrieu, Karg-Elert, Pachelbel, Schroeder).

——Alain. HADYN SOCIETY HSL 148 (*see* S. 532).

——Nowakowski. TELEFUNKEN LGX 66059 (*see* S. 533).

PRELUDE AND FUGUE IN C MINOR, S. 546

Prelude: Leipzig, about 1730; Fugue: Weimar, about 1716. A big, symphonic Prelude and a somewhat less imposing Fugue. Walcha's is the preferred version here, especially for the transparency of the counterpoint, unmatched in other recordings of this work.

——Walcha. ARCHIVE ARC 3018 (*see* S. 544).

——Schweitzer. COLUMBIA 5SL 223 (*see* S. 533).

——Marchal. LONDON DTL 93056 (*see* S. 537).

——(Prelude only) Commette. ANGEL 35368 (*see* S. 533).

PRELUDE AND FUGUE IN C, S. 547

Leipzig, about 1744. Whether one prefers the Schweitzer or the Walcha will depend on whether one agrees with the former's conception of the Prelude as "the vision of a crowd moving along in solemn jubilation," or the latter's interpretation of it as a kind of pastorale, with the gentle swing characteristic of that genre. My own preference is for Walcha, chiefly because of the lovelier sound of the Fugue in his recording. Cochereau's Fugue is sluggish, and the sound of his instrument comparatively harsh.

——Walcha. ARCHIVE ARC 3019 (with S. 548, 551, 565).

——Schweitzer. COLUMBIA 5SL 223 (*see* S. 533).

——Cochereau. OISEAU-LYRE OL 50125 (*see* S. 533).

PRELUDE AND FUGUE IN E MINOR, S. 548

Leipzig, between 1727 and 1736. Another of the gigantic pairs. The Prelude is long but crammed with interesting passages. The mighty Fugue, sometimes called the "Wedge" from the shape of its subject, is even longer, and of a rather unusual form for a fugue, in that the third of its three sections is a repetition of the first. Walcha is far out in front here, since the Richter is dull, the Alain recording is marred by her use of coarse-toned pedal stops in the Prelude, and the Eggington reverberation frequently dissolves the music into a whirring mixture of sounds.

——Walcha. ARCHIVE ARC 3019 (*see* S. 547).
——Richter. LONDON LL 1175 (*see* S. 542).
——Eggington. OISEAU-LYRE OL 50012 (*see* S. 532).
——Alain. HAYDN SOCIETY HSL 148 (*see* S. 532).

PRELUDE AND FUGUE IN G, S. 550

Weimar, about 1709, if not earlier at Arnstadt. The Prelude is a cheerful composition of no great depth; the Fugue starts out merrily too, but goes on for quite a while after the young Bach has squeezed all the juice out of it.

——Walcha. ARCHIVE ARC 3018 (*see* S. 544).

PRELUDE AND FUGUE IN A MINOR, S. 551

Arnstadt, before 1706, or possibly Lüneburg, 1700-1703. An early work not very well unified but containing some interesting and expressive material.

——Walcha. ARCHIVE ARC 3019 (*see* S. 547).

PRELUDE AND FUGUE IN E FLAT, S. 552

Published 1739. It is unlikely that Bach intended these two great works to be played as a pair. The Prelude introduces that wonderful collection of compositions on the chorale, Part III of the *Clavierübung* (*see below* under S. 669-689), and the Fugue (known as *St. Anne's* in England) rounds it off. Two sturdier pillars would be hard to find. Unfortunately none of the recordings is completely satisfactory. The Biggs performance is a strong one, but there are passages that are nothing but confusion. Perhaps the registrations chosen were not the clearest for recording purposes, or possibly the engineers could not catch the sounds clearly. The Weinrich Prelude lacks tension. Litaize, in an attempt to achieve monumentality in the Prelude, succeeds only in producing coarse, bloated noises among which the ear struggles to discern definite pitches. Walcha sacrifices monumentality in the Prelude for rhythmic verve, but in the middle section employs some of the wheezier stops in his otherwise fine old instrument. Marchal offers a majestic performance of the Prelude, but his Fugue plods along for a while before it picks up momentum. The Dupré version is much too reverberant for my taste.

——Walcha. Prelude: ARCHIVE ARC 3022 (with chorale preludes). Fugue: ARCHIVE ARC 3024 (with chorale preludes).

——André Marchal. Unicorn UNLP 1046 (with 6 chorale preludes).

——Marcel Dupré. Overtone 14 (with Mozart: Fantasia in F minor, K. 608; Adagio and Allegro in F minor, K. 594).

——Weinrich. WESTMINSTER WN 2205 (with S. 669-689). Two 12-in.

——Biggs. COLUMBIA ML 4097 (*see* S. 540).

——Litaize. LONDON DTL 93037 (*see* S. 536).

LITTLE PRELUDES AND FUGUES (8), S. 553-560

Weimar, before 1710. Biggs plays with his customary dexterity and rhythmic liveliness, though some listeners may find his invariable retards and

holding of final chords rather excessive. Each piece is played on a different European organ (five in Germany and one each in Austria, Holland, and Alsace) and Columbia's engineers have had considerable success in capturing the sound of the various instruments with clarity and realism.
——Biggs. COLUMBIA ML 5078 (with S. 572).

FANTASY IN C MINOR, S. 562

Weimar, between 1712 and 1716, if not later at Cöthen. An expressive work whose pathos is well conveyed by Commette, *doyen* of French organists, employing a nineteenth-century organ, and Walcha, playing the Schnitger at Cappel. Alain is handicapped by the sound of her instrument here. In the Heiller there are passages where it is hard to hear the top voices.
——Walcha. ARCHIVE ARC 3017 (*see* S. 541).
——Commette. ANGEL 35368 (*see* S. 533).
——Alain. HAYDN SOCIETY HSL 120 (*see* S. 525-530).
——Heiller. EPIC LC 3367 (*see* S. 538).

TOCCATA, ALLEGRO, AND FUGUE IN C, S. 564

Weimar, about 1709. The Biggs stands out above all the others. His Toccata has pert humor and a good deal of fantasy; his Adagio is properly grave but not dull; his Fugue is a virtuoso accomplishment, full of *brio*. Acceptable performances are given by Weinrich, who chooses a rather clanky stop for the melody of the Adagio and whose Fugue could do with a little more snap, and by Walcha, whose Toccata, after the pedal solo, is somewhat too brisk. The Marchal version, an excellent one, is played on his studio organ in Paris, which, while generously endowed, cannot be compared with the larger instruments. The others have their good points but are not recommended because of various weaknesses in performance or recording.

——Biggs. COLUMBIA ML 4284 (with S. 645-650).

——Weinrich. WESTMINSTER W-LAB 7047 (with S. 582). Or WESTMINSTER XWN 18260 (*see* S. 540).

——Walcha. ARCHIVE ARC 3020 (*see* S. 534).

——Marchal. Zodiac 335 (with 12 chorale preludes).

——Schweitzer. COLUMBIA SL 175 (*see* S. 531).

——Demessieux. LONDON LL 946 (*see* S. 543).

——Eggington. OISEAU-LYRE OL 50012 (*see* S. 532).

——Steinhaus. BOSTON B 1700 (*see* S. 532).

——Feike Asma. EPIC LC 3025 (with S. 582, chorale preludes; Handel: *Basso ostinato* from Concerto in G minor).

TOCCATA AND FUGUE IN D MINOR, S. 565

Weimar, about 1709, or possibly earlier in Arnstadt. This most popular of Bach's organ works was written as a display piece. The extraordinary effectiveness of the Toccata has made it a favorite with the virtuosos, and there is not a really bad performance in the list. So well do the first five organists listed below play that the reader will have to make his choice on the basis of the instrument used, other works included on the disk, price, or something of that sort. If hi-fi is his chief interest, he will find the greatest extremes of dynamics captured by Cook in the Foort recording. For me, the fi is quite hi enough in the better performance by Weinrich on the Westminster Laboratory record. The choice of organs is even greater than is implied by the number of editions. E. P. Biggs on Columbia 5032 performs the Toccata alone on thirteen European instruments and the Toccata and Fugue on a fourteenth. Specifications of all fourteen are given. This disk should be of special interest to organists. There seems to be no point in discussing the failings of the last ten performances; in most of them, as has been indicated, the weaknesses are minor.

——Weinrich. WESTMINSTER W-LAB 7023 or XWN 18260 (*see* S. 540).

——Biggs. COLUMBIA ML 4500 (with S. 578, 582, 596, App. 90).

——Walcha. ARCHIVE ARC 3019 (*see* S. 547).

——Heiller. EPIC LC 3132 (*see* S. 532).

——Heitmann. TELEFUNKEN LGX 66038 (*see* S. 543).

——Schweitzer. COLUMBIA 5SL 223 (*see* S. 533).

——Commette. ANGEL 35368 (*see* S. 533).

——Richter. LONDON LL 1174 (with S. 582, chorale prelude; Liszt: Prelude and Fugue on BACH).

——Fox. RCA VICTOR LM 1963 (*see* S. 532).

——Nowakowski. TELEFUNKEN LGX 66059 (*see* S. 533).

——Litaize. LONDON DTL 93037 (*see* S. 536).

——Coci. VOX DL 210 (see S. 543).

——Demessieux. LONDON LL 319 (*see* S. 532).

——Reginald Foort. COOK 10545 (with works by Boellmann, Dubois, Handel, Reubke).

——Biggs. COLUMBIA ML 5032.

——(Toccata only) Biggs. COLUMBIA SL 219 (with works by Buxtehude, Purcell, Sweelinck, Pachelbel). Two 12-in.

TOCCATA IN E, S. 566

Arnstadt, about 1707. One of the less interesting works, with an undistinguished first section and a dull fugue on a long and unadventurous subject. A second fugue is somewhat better, but by no means up to Bach's highest standard. Weinrich is clearer than Heiller and not so ponderous in the first section. Walcha, strangely, plays only the first two of the four sections.

——Weinrich. WESTMINSTER WN 14148 (*see* S. 538).

——Heiller. EPIC LC 3132 (*see* S. 532).

——Walcha. ARCHIVE ARC 3020 (*see* S. 534).

PRELUDE IN A MINOR, S. 569

Weimar, about 1709 or possibly earlier, in Arnstadt. A mechanically constructed piece of no great interest.

——Heiller. EPIC LC 3367 (*see* S. 538).

FANTASY IN G, S. 572

Arnstadt, 1705-1706, if not later in Weimar. The lordly stride of a central section for five voices (*Gravement*) is flanked by improvisational sections. The choice here, I think, is between Viderø and Walcha, depending upon whether one takes the marking of the opening, "*Très vitement*," seriously, as Viderø does, or agrees with Schweitzer, as Walcha seems to, that it is not to be observed too strictly. The Heitmann is a good performance, too; the only drawback there is the absence of bands between pieces on the disk. Alain is acceptable.

Nowakowski has a thick, heavy registration in the *Gravement*. Biggs, for once, is badly recorded: the piece is a blur (not so the others on the same disk, however).

——Viderø. HAYDN SOCIETY HSL 128 (*see* S. 536).

——Walcha. ARCHIVE ARC 3020 (*see* S. 534).

——Heitmann. TELEFUNKEN LGX 66009 (with S. 590, 769; works by Böhm, Walther, Buxtehude).

——Alain. HAYDN SOCIETY HSL 120 (*see* S. 525-530).

——Nowakowski. TELEFUNKEN LGM 65030 or LGX 66059 (*see* S. 533).

——Biggs. COLUMBIA ML 5078 (*see* S. 553-560).

FUGUE IN G, S. 577

Arnstadt, 1705-1706. A jolly fugue in the rhythm of a gigue. Fox's virtuoso performance surpasses the other in clarity as well as speed.

——Fox. RCA VICTOR LM 1963 (*see* S. 532).

——Demessieux. LONDON LL 946 (*see* S. 543).

FUGUE IN G MINOR, S. 578

Weimar, about 1709, or possibly earlier in Arnstadt. This lovely Fugue is sometimes called "the little G minor" to distinguish it from S. 542. Biggs's performance is a model of clarity and good taste. So is Walcha's but his tempo seems a shade slow. Nunez races through the work and everything sounds blurred.

——Biggs. COLUMBIA ML 4500 (*see* S. 565).

——Walcha. ARCHIVE ARC 3021 (with S. 582, 588-590).

——Nunez. COOK 1056 (*see* S. 542).

PASSACAGLIA AND FUGUE IN C MINOR, S. 582

Weimar, 1716-1717, if not later in Cöthen. Of this famous masterpiece there are no completely impressive recordings but several satisfactory ones. Weinrich (in one of the Westminster pressings), Walcha, Biggs, and Litaize all perform well and are recorded well enough, and the choice among them boils down to a preference among organs or among registration schemes. The recording of Schweitzer suffers from the usual lack of sharpness, and there is distortion in the final variation. Richter is rather metronomic and soporific. Heiller's performance differs from most in that it begins strongly, thus detracting somewhat from the power of the later climaxes. Asma has moments of blur, his last variations sound coarse, and he maintains a high dynamic level going into the Fugue, which consequently remains unrelievedly loud. By changing registration too frequently Nowakowski gives an impression of fussiness. Miss Coci, on the other hand, even though she has some nine hundred stops to draw on (in the West Point organ), exercises remarkable restraint in that respect. She does, however, feel impelled to repeat part of the last measure of the last variation.

——Weinrich. WESTMINSTER W-LAB 7047 (see S. 564) or XWN 18260 (see S. 540).

——Walcha. ARCHIVE ARC 3021 (see S. 578).

——Biggs. COLUMBIA ML 4500 (see S. 565).

——Litaize. LONDON DTL 93037 (see S. 536).

——Weinrich. M-G-M E 3021 (with S. 593, 645-650, 2 chorale preludes).

——Schweitzer. COLUMBIA 5SL 223 (see S. 533).

——Heiller. Epic lc 3261 (*see* S. 531).
——Asma. Epic lc 3025 (*see* S. 564).
——Coci. Vox dl 210 (*see* S. 543).
——Richter. London ll 1174 (*see* S. 565).
——Nowakowski. Telefunken lgm 65030 or lgx 66059 (*see* S. 533).

Canzona in D minor, S. 588

Weimar, about 1709. This richly melancholy, chromatic piece sounds most affecting, it seems to me, under the hands of Walcha, although the other two performances are unexceptionable.
——Walcha. Archive arc 3021 (*see* S. 578).
——Weinrich. Westminster wn 18148 (*see* S. 538).
——Schweitzer. Columbia sl 175 (*see* S. 531).

Allabreve in D, S. 589

Weimar, about 1709. A work that is rather low in expressivity, though quite high in contrapuntal skill. Walcha treats it as a contemplative piece; Weinrich and Heiller attempt to make a majestic thing of it and choose registrations of unrelieved heaviness.
——Walcha. Archive arc 3021 (*see* S. 578).
——Weinrich. Westminster wn 18148 (*see* S. 538).
——Heiller. Epic lc 3132 (*see* S. 532).

Pastorale in F, S. 590

Arnstadt, between 1703 and 1707, or possibly later in Weimar. A charming set of four pieces, of which only the first is a pastorale. Perhaps the best all-round version is Heitmann's even though his instrument is less than perfect. Unfortunately, one

has to know the music to find it on this Telefunken disk, which has no visible separation between compositions. The other performances are good too, but Viderø's first movement is rather darkly colored, Walcha's third sounds a little too fluty, and in the Pastorale proper one can barely hear the music played on the manuals in the Alain recording.
——Heitmann. TELEFUNKEN LGX 66009 (*see* S. 572).
——Viderø. HAYDN SOCIETY HSL 128 (*see* S. 536).
——Walcha. ARCHIVE ARC 3021 (*see* S. 578).
——Alain. HAYDN SOCIETY HSL 120 (*see* S. 525-530).

CONCERTO AFTER VIVALDI, IN A MINOR, S. 593

Weimar, between 1708 and 1717; based on Vivaldi's Op. 3, No. 8. The Weinrich recording is not ideal—among other things, the thumping of keys can be plainly heard in the Adagio and beginning of the finale—but it has no competition. There is much reverberation in tutti passages of the Nunez, and the finale is lacking. The Prince-Joseph disk is interesting only because it presents a pedal harpsichord.
——Weinrich. M-G-M E 3021 (*see* S. 582).
——Nunez. COOK 1056 (*see* S. 542).
——Prince-Joseph. COOK 11312 (*see* S. 541).

CONCERTO AFTER VIVALDI, IN D MINOR, S. 596

Weimar, between 1708 and 1717; based on Vivaldi's Op. 3, No. 11. The fine Largo is especially effective in this performance.
——Biggs. COLUMBIA ML 4500 (*see* S. 565).

ORGELBUECHLEIN, S. 599-644

Partly at Weimar, 1708-1717, partly at Cöthen, 1717-1723. The *Little Organ Book*, which may have been written for Wilhelm Friedemann Bach, is a collection of forty-five settings of chorale melodies grouped mostly according to the liturgical seasons. Most of them are quite short. All of them repay careful listening and study, for Bach loved the old tunes and these brief settings are the quintessence of their meaning for him. In order to grasp this meaning fully, it is necessary, as Schweitzer has pointed out, that we know what each chorale is about. In this respect Biggs's notes for his own album are most helpful; they not only discuss each work individually but include the score of the whole *Orgelbüchlein*. His performance in general is as penetrating and as poetic as any of the others, and in some preludes more so. I would therefore not hesitate to put his set at the head of my list if it were not for one peculiarity. In this album each of Bach's settings is preceded by a playing of the chorale simply, but fully, harmonized. The impact of Bach's wonderful setting is thus weakened: its principal melody and basic harmonies have already been heard; and instead of being an independent little poem, it becomes a mere variation. The other three performances are all generally satisfactory, and the choice among them is again mostly a matter of instrument and registration. Both Viderø and Weinrich supply a list of their registrations for each chorale prelude.

——Walcha. ARCHIVE ARC 3025/6. Two 12-in.
——Weinrich. WESTMINSTER WN 2203. Two 12-in.

——Viderø. HAYDN SOCIETY HSL D. Two 12-in.
——Biggs. COLUMBIA KLS 227. Three 12-in.

SIX CHORALES OF VARIOUS SORTS (SCHUEBLER), S. 645-650

Published by J. G. Schübler in 1746. Five of these settings are transcribed by Bach from cantatas of his. All six are magnificent examples of his skill at coiling freely invented melodies around the trunks of sturdy old chorales. Once more, as in the *Orgelbüchlein*, Biggs's performance would have been completely satisfactory if he had not prefaced each piece by a richly harmonized version of the chorale. This is of little use as a mnemonic device here: Bach always splits up the chorale into its constituent phrases. On the other hand, Biggs (like Walcha and Weinrich) is always careful to make the chorale phrases, when they do appear, stand out clearly, so that his preliminary statement of the chorale is not only confusing but superfluous. How much better it would have been if he had been content to print the chorale melody in the notes, so that one could follow it while listening to Bach's setting. Walcha and Weinrich are quite acceptable; I happen to prefer the sound of the small organ of Saint Jakobi at Lübeck to that of the Princeton University Chapel organ.

——Walcha. ARCHIVE ARC 3029 (with S. 665-668).
——Weinrich. M-G-M E 3021 (*see* S. 582).
——Biggs. COLUMBIA ML 4284 (*see* S. 564).
——(S. 646, 648, 650 only) Unnamed organist. AEOLIAN-SKINNER Vol. II (*see* S. 525).

CHORALES (18) OF VARIOUS SORTS, S. 651-668

Composed at various times and rewritten at Leipzig, 1747-1750, Bach intended to publish these chorales as a set. The meditations on the chorale, as elaborate and as beautiful as the Schübler set, show Bach's enormous skill and blazing imagination at their maturest. Sometimes he puts the chorale tune in one voice, sometimes in another; sometimes he breaks it up among the various voices. But each time, no matter how the piece is constructed, it is suffused with the feeling of the words that originally accompanied the tune. The set includes such masterpieces as *Schmücke dich, o liebe Seele* and *An Wasserflüssen Babylon* as well as Bach's last composition, *Vor deinen Thron tret' ich*. All are superbly played by Walcha.

——Walcha. ARCHIVE ARC 3027/9 (with S. 645-650). Three 12-in.

COMPOSITIONS ON THE CHORALE, FROM THE "CLAVIERUEBUNG," PART III, S. 669-689

Published 1739. These twenty-one settings of ten chorales are described in the title of the first edition as "Various Preludes on the Catechism and Other Hymns." In that edition and in the present recordings they are introduced by the splendid Prelude in E-flat, S. 552, and rounded out by its giant triple Fugue. Both performers set the chorale tunes off neatly by their registration whenever this is feasible, and exploit the variety of color obtainable on the fine old organs they use. Westminster lists the registration for each setting.

——Walcha. ARCHIVE ARC 3022/4 (with S. 552 and 5 miscellaneous chorale preludes). Three 12-in.
——Weinrich. WESTMINSTER WN 2205 (*see* S. 552).

FUGA SOPRA IL MAGNIFICAT, S. 733

A powerful work, played with appropriate brilliance.
——Walcha. ARCHIVE ARC 3030 (with S. 768, 769).

PARTITE DIVERSE SOPRA O GOTT, DU FROMMER GOTT, S. 767

Lüneburg, about 1700, if not earlier in Ohrdruf. This boyhood work is in nine sections, the first a harmonization of the chorale, the other eight variations on it. Well performed by both artists.
——Viderø. HAYDN SOCIETY HSL 94 (with S. 769, 11 chorale preludes).
——Marchal. Unicorn UNLP 1048 (with 3 chorale preludes; works by Sweelinck, A. Gabrieli, Cabezón, Purcell, Buxtehude).

PARTITE DIVERSE SOPRA SEI GEGRUESSET, JESU GUETIG, S. 768

Bach worked on this set of variations at various times during his career. The result is not entirely happy: of the eleven variations eight (including the last) are short, the first and ninth are somewhat longer, and the tenth is very long—a lopsided layout; and many of them, alas, are dull. They are less so, however, in Walcha's imaginative treatment than in Heiller's relatively workaday performance.
——Walcha. ARCHIVE ARC 3030 (*see* S. 733).
——Heiller. EPIC LC 3261 (*see* S. 531).

CANONIC VARIATIONS ON VOM HIMMEL HOCH, DA KOMM' ICH HER, S. 769

Leipzig 1746-1747, on the occasion of Bach's admission to the "Society of Musical Sciences." A tour de force of craftsmanship. In five movements Bach constructs as many different kinds of canons over or under or around the Christmas chorale. Heitmann's performance has the most vitality, Viderø's instrument the least attractive sound. You have to grope around on the Telefunken disk to find the beginning of this work, because there are no bands. The Haydn Society lists the registrations employed.
——Heitmann. TELEFUNKEN LGX 66009 (*see* S. 572).
——Walcha. ARCHIVE ARC 3030 (*see* S. 733).
——Viderø. HAYDN SOCIETY HSL 94 (*see* S. 767).

FUGUE IN C, S. APP. 90

This rather uninteresting piece based on a fanfare-like subject is listed by Schmieder among the doubtful works.
——Biggs. COLUMBIA ML 4500 (*see* S. 565).

CLAVIER WORKS

TWO-PART INVENTIONS (15), S. 772-786
Cöthen, 1720-1723. These marvelous little demonstrations of what genius can do with meager means are played by Landowska with a maximum of elo-

quence and a minimum of sentimentality. She adds many ornaments, but they are always in perfect taste. Eloquence is also achieved in Kirkpatrick's more sober reading, which has the advantage of employing the clavichord, probably the type of instrument, capable of certain nuances of dynamics and phrasing not obtainable on the eighteenth-century harpsichord, that Bach had in mind. Present-day listeners must decide for themselves whether its sound pleases them. The volume control should be set considerably lower than normally if the tone of the clavichord is not to be exaggeratedly magnified. Friskin's performance is neat and conventional.

——Wanda Landowska, harpsichord. RCA VICTOR LM 1974 (with Clavier Concerto in D minor).

——Ralph Kirkpatrick, clavichord. CONCERT HALL CHS 1088. 10-in.

——James Friskin, piano. VANGUARD BG 543/5 (with S. 814-817, 903, 904, 906, 911, 944, 971, 992). Three 12-in.

[——Erno Balogh, piano. LYRICHORD 1 (with 18 preludes).]

THREE-PART SYMPHONIES (15), S. 787-801

Cöthen, 1720-1723. Both pianists play simply and straightforwardly. With Balogh there is never any question of which of the three voices is most important at the moment. Foss is less didactic and a little more subtle. Neither player, it seems to me, does full justice to the fantasy in these pieces. A definite advantage of the Decca disk is that there is a band after every "symphony."

——Lukas Foss, piano. DECCA DL 9634.

———Balogh, piano. Lyrichord ll 2 (with S. 802-805).

Duets (4) from the Clavieruebung, Part III, S. 802-805

Published 1739. These gravely beautiful works, in two parts but constructed on a considerably larger scale than the Inventions, deserve to be better known than they are. The Walcha performance is more serene, the Balogh more emphatic.

———Walcha, harpsichord. Lyrichord ll 2 (see S. 787-801).

———Balogh, piano. Lyrichord ll 2 (see S. 787-801).

English Suites (6), S. 806-811

Cöthen, before 1722. Like the French Suites, these contain some delightful dances, but unlike the other group, they also contain some long and weighty preludes, and even some of the dances have a subjective emotional quality. Kirkpatrick's performance is masterly. His fast tempos are lively but not hurried; his slow ones do not drag. His embellishments always sound natural and in good taste. In the second and third suites the score presents two versions of the Sarabande: one a relatively unadorned one, and the other with added embellishments. Kirkpatrick plays through the movement once with repeats, then plays the embellished version, without repeats. This is not in accordance with his custom on the concert platform, where he is much more likely to use the embellished version for the repeat of each section (as do the other performers listed). The Archive version is no doubt a result of that company's insistence on comprehensiveness.

Valenti's performance is also praiseworthy, if not up to Kirkpatrick's in insight and flexibility. Gianoli is better here than in the French Suites. Her tempos are more plausible and she is not as impervious to nuance as she seems to be there. The Archive has bands between movements, a convenience not to be found in either of the Westminster sets.

Gulda's performance of No. 3 has much to recommend it for those who want an English Suite played on the piano. Restout's version of No. 4, though different from Kirkpatrick's and Valenti's in matters of tempo and spirit, is not without its points of interest, including her treatment of the Allemande, where she applies unwritten dotted rhythms. Backhaus' playing of No. 6 is disappointingly superficial.

——Kirkpatrick, harpsichord. ARCHIVE ARC 3068/70. Three 12-in.

——Fernando Valenti, harpsichord. WESTMINSTER XWN 18384/5. Two 12-in.

——Reine Gianoli, piano. WESTMINSTER XWN 18382/3. Two 12-in.

——(No. 3, in G minor, S. 808) Friedrich Gulda, piano. LONDON LL 756 (with S. 877; Mozart: Sonata in A minor, K. 310; Rondo in D, K. 485).

——(No. 4, in F, S. 809) Denise Restout, harpsichord. R.E.B. 1 (with S. 813).

——(No. 6, in D minor, S. 811) Wilhelm Backhaus, piano. LONDON LL 1638 (with S. 816, 860, 884).

FRENCH SUITES (6), S. 812-817

First five suites composed at Cöthen, 1722. It is not easy to choose between the two performances on the harpsichord. Ahlgrimm fluctuates more widely than Valenti: when she is imaginative, she is more imaginative than he is; when she is not, she is much more mechanical. Her rhythm is not as firm as his, it is more improvisational, more flexible; and she does not hesitate in some of the sarabandes and elsewhere to apply the dotted rhythms of baroque practice. On the other hand, she omits most of the repeats. This enables her to get all six works onto one disk, but it makes many of the movements sound incomplete. Both the piano versions are very neat and rather dull. Borovsky's fast movements are crisp and immaculate but usually perfunctory. Gianoli's, when they aren't too hurried, sound like finger exercises. In the slow movements neither pianist reveals much poetry.

——Fernando Valenti, harpsichord. WESTMINSTER xwn 18157/8. Two 12-in.

——Isolde Ahlgrimm, harpsichord. COLUMBIA ML 4746.

——Alexander Borovsky, piano. VOX PL 8192. Two 12-in.

——Reine Gianoli, piano. WESTMINSTER xwn 18155/6. Two 12-in.

FRENCH SUITE NO. 2, IN C MINOR, S. 813

The lovely Allemande is played poetically by Valenti, who sticks to the score, and by Restout, who does not but treats rhythm and ornamentation very freely, as was probably done in Bach's time. Valenti's Gigue, on the other hand, is rather ungainly and heavy; it is more graceful under the fingers of Ahlgrimm and Restout.

——Valenti, harpsichord. WESTMINSTER xwn 18157.

——Restout, harpsichord. R.E.B. 1 (see S. 806-811).
——Ahlgrimm, harpsichord. COLUMBIA ML 4746.
——Borovsky, piano. VOX PL 8192.
——Gianoli, piano. WESTMINSTER XWN 18155.

FRENCH SUITE NO. 3, IN B MINOR, S. 814

Valenti plays the Anglaise after the Minuet instead of before (some editions print it one way, some the other). Again he plays the Gigue in a rather heavy registration; Ahlgrimm's is less ponderous. Gianoli hurries through the Courante and her Sarabande is wooden. Among the piano versions, Friskin's is a bit more colorful than Borovsky's.
——Ahlgrimm, harpsichord. COLUMBIA ML 4746.
——Valenti, harpsichord. WESTMINSTER XWN 18157.
——Friskin, piano. VANGUARD BG 543/5 (see S. 772-786).
——Borovsky, piano. VOX PL 8192.
——Gianoli, piano. WESTMINSTER XWN 18155.

FRENCH SUITE NO. 4, IN E FLAT, S. 815

Valenti seems most satisfactory here, his tender treatment of the Sarabande being especially outstanding. None of the pianists distinguishes himself particularly, although Borovsky builds the opening of the Allemande nicely and Gianoli's Gigue is the brightest of the three.
——Valenti, harpsichord. WESTMINSTER XWN 18158.
——Ahlgrimm, harpsichord. COLUMBIA ML 4746.
——Gianoli, piano. WESTMINSTER XWN 18156.
——Borovsky, piano. VOX PL 8192.
——Friskin, piano. VANGUARD BG 543/5 (see S. 772-786).

FRENCH SUITE NO. 5, IN G, S. 816

All seven artists play the familiar Gavotte well, and all but one do justice to the jolly Gigue: only Gianoli manages to make it sound rigid. Ahlgrimm imparts a special snap to the Sarabande and Loure by holding the dotted notes longer than their written values, in accordance with baroque practice. A few split notes in the Demus.

——Ahlgrimm, harpsichord. COLUMBIA ML 4746.
——Valenti, harpsichord. WESTMINSTER XWN 18158.
——Backhaus, piano. LONDON LL 1638 (*see* S. 811).
——Jörg Demus, piano. REMINGTON RLP 199-25 (with S. 825).
——Friskin, piano. VANGUARD BG 543/5 (*see* S. 772-786).
——Borovsky, piano. VOX PL 8192.
——Gianoli, piano. WESTMINSTER XWN 18156.

FRENCH SUITE NO. 6, IN E, S. 817

The charming Allemande of this, the most familiar of the French Suites, has a fine lyric flow under Valenti's fingers. Gianoli plays it too fast and Ahlgrimm too deliberately. The latter, however, again enlivens the dotted rhythms of the Sarabande. Friskin plays the Minuet after the Bourrée instead of before it, perhaps in order not to follow the Bourrée by another fast movement, the Gigue.

——Valenti, harpsichord. WESTMINSTER XWN 18158.
——Ahlgrimm, harpsichord. COLUMBIA ML 4746.
——Friskin, piano. VANGUARD BG 543/5 (*see* S. 772-786).
——Borovsky, piano. VOX PL 8192.
——Gianoli, piano. WESTMINSTER XWN 18156.

PARTITAS (6), S. 825-830.

Published 1726-1730. These fine suites consist of dance movements, each set being introduced, like the English Suites, by a prelude of some kind. The variety of shape and character Bach managed to give to those preludes, and indeed to each of the dance patterns, is astonishing. There is unfortunately no satisfactory performance employing a harpsichord. Three of the partitas, to be sure, are played on that instrument in the Remington album, but the performances are so stiff that they cannot be considered here. Tureck, Jambor, and Badura-Skoda illustrate the pianist's dilemma mentioned in the prefatory remarks to this section. Tureck plays with more nuance, on the whole, in dynamics, touch, and phrasing. It is a thoroughly pianistic style and probably corresponds, one imagines, to the best type of Bach playing in the early nineteenth century. Jambor's color range is considerably less wide, and she consequently holds the attention less consistently, although she will sometimes choose a better tempo, as in the Sarabande of No. 2. The Royale surfaces are poorer than Capitol's but Tureck's are the only disks on which the individual movements are separated by bands. The young Badura-Skoda seems to be aiming in the right direction, but he often sounds as though he were playing a carefully learned lesson. Demus is rather dull on the whole; the only vital performance in the Remington album is Sari Biro's of No. 2.

——Rosalyn Tureck, piano. ROYALE 1415/8. Four 12-in.

——Agi Jambor, piano. CAPITOL PBR 8344. Two 12-in.

——Paul Badura-Skoda, piano. Westminster xwn 3307. Three 12-in $11.95. (xwn 18376/8.)
——Jörg Demus, piano (Nos. 1 and 6); Sari Biro, piano (No. 2); John Gillespie, harpsichord (Nos. 3-5). Remington r 199-108/3. Three 12-in.

Partita No. 1, in B-flat, S. 825

Landowska's Prelude is heavy-footed toward the end; in the Courante she chooses to interpret the dotted-eighths-and-sixteenths (against triplets) as exactly that, instead of playing the sixteenth with the last eighth of the triplet, in the baroque manner; in the Sarabande she adds chords. Her divagations from the score are not convincing re-creations here, as they are so often elsewhere, but seem merely to be willful changes. Lipatti is clean, sensible, and pleasant. There is little interpretative difference between his two performances; the recording is a little better in the Columbia; the Angel is part of a recording of Lipatti's last recital. Badura-Skoda, Jambor, Demus, and Kitain are respectable but not very interesting (the last-named plays on an early nineteenth-century piano). Tureck performs with style, and tries to achieve variety of shading and color; but her Prelude drags slightly and she is the victim of a mannerism —almost every final chord is rolled, with an appoggiatura.
——Dinu Lipatti, piano. Columbia ml 4633 (with Bach transcriptions; Mozart: Sonata in A minor, K. 310). Or Angel 3556B (with same Mozart Sonata; Schubert: Impromptus Nos. 2 and 3; Chopin: 13 Waltzes). Two 12-in.
——Landowska, harpsichord. RCA Victor lct 1137 (with S. 903, 912, 971).

——Badura-Skoda, piano. WESTMINSTER XWN 3307 or XWN 18376.

——Tureck, piano. ROYALE 1415.

——Jambor, piano. CAPITOL PBR 8344.

——Demus, piano. REMINGTON RLP 199-25 (*see* S. 816) and R 199-108/3.

——Anatol Kitain, piano. ESOTERIC ESP 3001 (with Bach transcriptions).

PARTITA No. 4, IN D, S. 828

The Gillespie, the only performance on a harpsichord, is unfortunately the least interesting, being as regular and as unyielding as a metronome throughout. The late William Kapell, on the other hand, did a fine job with this Partita—surprisingly, for Bach was far from a specialty of his. In the Allemande and Sarabande he sings the long phrases with the suppleness and sensitivity of a great vocalist. Unfortunately the Gigue is omitted. It is precisely in the Allemande and Sarabande that Jambor has the least to contribute; she does much better with the livelier Courante and Gigue. Badura-Skoda, despite some sensitive playing, is not very convincing. The most acceptable complete performance is Tureck's, although with the usual reservation about the authenticity of her style.

——Tureck, piano. ROYALE 1416.

——Jambor, piano. CAPITOL PBR 8344.

——Badura-Skoda, piano. WESTMINSTER XWN 3307 or XWN 18377.

——William Kapell, piano. RCA VICTOR LM 1791 (with works by Schubert and Liszt).

——Gillespie, harpsichord. REMINGTON R 199-108/3.

PARTITA NO. 5, IN G, S. 829

Gould's tempos are on the whole more rapid than Tureck's, but except in the Corrente he is quite convincing. And the other movements have under his hands a polish and grace and character that stamp this as Bach playing of the first order. Faint humming by the pianist is only occasionally audible.

——Glenn Gould, piano. COLUMBIA ML 5186 (with Partita No. 6).

——Tureck, piano. ROYALE 1417.

——Jambor, piano. CAPITOL PBR 8344.

——Badura-Skoda, piano. WESTMINSTER XWN 3307 or XWN 18378.

——Gillespie, harpsichord. REMINGTON R 199-108/3.

PARTITA NO. 6, IN E MINOR, S. 830

Gieseking plays the great Toccata in a rather matter-of-fact way. In the other movements he favors fast tempos—he makes a virtuoso exercise out of the Courante; altogether his reading is more interesting as a study in finger control than as a representation of Bach. Gould is again poetic and imaginative, and has a way of making the ornaments seem inevitable. There is not much to choose as between Tureck and Jambor; in the Toccata, Tureck stresses the drama, Jambor the pathos. After a strong opening in the Toccata, Badura-Skoda relapses into the neutral style that predominates in his playing of the whole set. Demus is respectable but rather insensitive.

——Gould, piano. COLUMBIA ML 5186.

——Tureck, piano. ROYALE 1418.

——Jambor, piano. CAPITOL PBR 8344.

——Badura-Skoda, piano. WESTMINSTER XWN 3307 or XWN 18378.

——Demus, piano. REMINGTON R 199-108/3. Or REMINGTON R 199-92 (with 2 preludes and fugues from *The Well-Tempered Clavier*).

——Walter Gieseking, piano. COLUMBIA ML 4646 (with works by Handel and Scarlatti).

PARTITA IN B MINOR, S. 831

Published 1735. This elaborate suite comes from Part II of the *Clavierübung*, where it bears the title *Overture nach französischer Art*. It is ably performed here on a harpsichord made in England by Thomas Goff. Heller is a little overfond of showing off his instrument's generous endowments, but in general his playing is crisp and lively. Wollmann's is neat and rather superficial.

——Stanislav Heller, harpsichord. DELYSE EC 3135. 10-in.

——Eva Wollmann, piano. WESTMINSTER XWN 18105 (with S. 971, 989).

THE WELL-TEMPERED CLAVIER, S. 846-893

Part I: Cöthen, 1722; Part II: Leipzig, 1744. There is a belief, fostered by some reviewers, that Landowska takes great liberties with Bach's text. This is an exaggeration. The fact is that she never departs from the spirit of the text and seldom from the letter. When she does, it is usually in the ornamentation—a matter in which the manuscript sources are by no means always in agreement. What probably led to the belief is the freedom and flexibility of her phrasing. For while she is capable of iron rhythm when the music calls for it, her main concern is to be sure that the music sings and breathes naturally. That is why Bach is eloquent under her fingers, and not dreary or mechanical. There can never, fortunately, be a "definitive" performance of this, or any, masterwork; but Landowska has here set up a standard that for penetration and for all-round satisfactoriness will be hard to surpass.

Ahlgrimm is by no means devoid of temperament, and she does many of the preludes and fugues rather nicely. But with others she tends toward a grim ponderousness; and not all her attempts to achieve nuance are convincing. Some of them seem to arise, not from the natural flow of the music, but from a decision that it was time to be less metronomic and this was as good a place as any.

For those who must have Bach on a piano rather than a harpsichord, the Tureck is recommended. This thoughtful artist plays very clearly and with excellent control. In the fugues she displays a delicate balance in the weight of the individual voices that can be achieved only by a first-class pianist. Her tone is good, her ideas always interesting. Some of the preludes and fugues come off less well than others, but that is true (though more seldom) even with Landowska. Practically the only objection I have is to Miss Tureck's habit of ornamenting the final chord of a piece unnecessarily. Not only are such ornaments absent in the sources, but Miss Tureck does not even have the harpsichordist's excuse of being otherwise unable to sustain the chord for its full value. Demus' playing, while lacking this fault and being clean and beautifully controlled, is rather cool and stays on the surface. There is little intensity, little feeling for the inner life of a phrase.

——Landowska, harpsichord. RCA Victor lm 1017, 1107, 1136, 1152, 1708, 1820. Six 12-in.

——Tureck, piano. Decca dx 127 and 128. Two sets of three 12-in.

——Demus, piano. Westminster wn 5501 (with score). Five 12-in.

——(Book I only) Ahlgrimm, harpsichord. Columbia sl 191. Three 12-in.

Prelude and Fugue in A minor, S. 894

Weimar, about 1717. These brilliant pieces were later used by Bach in his Concerto for Clavier, Violin, Flute, and Strings, in A minor, S. 1044. They are neatly and smoothly played here.

——Jambor, piano. Capitol p 8348 (with S. 903, 971, 998).

Chromatic Fantasy and Fugue, S. 903

Weimar, about 1720; revised Leipzig, 1730. There is something to be said for every one of these performances. It is simply the misfortune of six of these artists that they are up against one of the great Bach performances of our time, one that belongs, in the reviewer's opinion, among the dozen best keyboard recordings ever made. Everyone here plays the Fugue well, but no one approaches Landowska in the Fantasy. Dramatic impact, unceasing eloquence, an improvisatory quality making each event sound new and unexpected, together with an over-all planning and control that keep the piece building up to the tragic power of the final measures—these are some of the elements of an incomparable reading. Valenti's is very good, but lacks the drive of Landowska's. Of the performances on a piano, Kempff's is perhaps the most interesting, as an example of the old romantic type of Bach interpretation at its best —an anachronism, but, taken on its own terms, magisterial and compelling. Jambor is by no means devoid of imagination; Friskin has traces of the romantic approach; Slenczynska is neat and thoughtful; Serkin, rather sober and in some passages surprisingly cut-and-dried.

——Landowska, harpsichord. RCA Victor lct 1137 (*see* S. 825).

——Valenti, harpsichord. Lyrichord ll 47 (with S. 911, 912).

——Wilhelm Kempff, piano. London ll 791 (with Bach transcriptions).

——Jambor, piano. Capitol p 8348 (*see* S. 894).

——Friskin, piano. Vanguard bg 543/5 (*see* S. 772-786).

——Ruth Slenczynska, piano. Music Library mlr 7030 (with S. 911, 963, 971).

——Rudolf Serkin, piano. Columbia ml 4350 (with S. 971; Sonata for Cello and Piano, in G minor).

Fantasy and Fugue in A minor, S. 904

Leipzig, about 1725. An unusually fine double fugue is the feature of this little-known work. Clear, straightforward performance.

——Friskin, piano. Vanguard bg 543/5 (*see* S. 772-786).

Fantasy in C minor, S. 906

Leipzig, about 1738. A chromatic work, intense and almost romantic in mood. Friskin's reading is a little more deliberate than Jambor's, but more effectively contrasts the middle portion of each section with its

beginning and end. In the manuscript this is joined by a fugue, which is regarded by some authorities as incomplete and is not played in these recordings.
——Friskin, piano. VANGUARD BG 543/5 (*see* S. 772-786).
——Jambor, piano. CAPITOL PBR 8354 (with S. 910-916, 920, 922). Two 12-in.

TOCCATAS, S. 910-916

All seven of Bach's toccatas are presented in the album listed below. Miss Jambor's playing is technically unexceptionable. Everything is neat and brisk. Some of the slow sections are taken a little too quickly and lose part of their effect, but the rest are nicely done. S. 911-914 will be dealt with individually, since there are several recordings of each. Here we may point out that in the Toccata in F-sharp minor, S. 910 (Cöthen, about 1720), while the introductory section could be more rhapsodic, the Presto is very cleanly played. Similarly, in the G major Toccata, S. 916 (Weimar, about 1709), although the Adagio seems a shade fast, the sunny gaiety of the Scarlattian opening and of the cheerful Fugue are well conveyed.
——Jambor, piano. CAPITOL PBR 8354 (*see* S. 906).

TOCCATA IN C MINOR, S. 911

Cöthen, about 1720. A solid, imposing work with a splendid fugue. Next to Valenti's pithy performance on the harpsichord, all the piano versions sound thin and pale. The most vital and imaginative of these is the one by young Casadesus. The differences among the rest are minor.

——Valenti, harpsichord. LYRICHORD LL 47 (*see* S. 903).

——Jean Casadesus, piano. ANGEL 45003 (with Clavier Concertos Nos. 1 and 5).

——Jambor, piano. CAPITOL PBR 8354 (*see* S. 906).

——Friskin, piano. VANGUARD BG 543/5 (*see* S. 772-786).

——Slenczynska, piano. MUSIC LIBRARY MLR 7030 (*see* S. 903).

TOCCATA IN D, S. 912

Weimar, about 1710. This is a rather sprawling work, for Bach, but it includes a playful allegro, a fine, brooding adagio, and a cheerful giguelike fugue. All three of the harpsichord versions are good on the whole. The Landowska seems just about right in every respect. Valenti has some heavy-handed moments in the Allegro and plays the Finale very fast; on his disk the Toccata is split between the sides. In the Marlowe, which is otherwise quite nice, there are passages in the Allegro where undue weight is given to the left-hand part. Of the performances on a piano, the Jambor is preferred, Bundervoët's being rather superficial.

——Landowska, harpsichord. RCA VICTOR LCT 1137 (*see* S. 825).

——Sylvia Marlowe, harpsichord. REMINGTON R 199-136 (with Scarlatti: 7 Sonatas; Couperin: *Les Folies Françaises*).

——Valenti, harpsichord. LYRICHORD LL 47 (*see* S. 903).

——Jambor, piano. CAPITOL PBR 8354 (*see* S. 906).

——Agnelle Bundervoët, piano. LONDON DTL 93051 (with S. 914, Chaconne, chorale prelude),

TOCCATA IN D MINOR, S. 913

Weimar, about 1710. Two improvisatory sections, each followed by a double fugue, make up this Toccata. The fugues are not especially interesting (the second one seems to have exhausted its material long before it comes to an end) but the other movements have a poetic quality, particularly when played as eloquently as Valenti plays them here. Both of the piano versions are acceptable.
——Valenti, harpsichord. LYRICHORD LL 48 (with S. 914, 998).
——Gianoli, piano. WESTMINSTER XWN 18100 (with S. 922, Chaconne).
——Jambor, piano. CAPITOL PBR 8354 (see S. 906).

TOCCATA IN E MINOR, S. 914

Weimar, about 1710. The early part of this Toccata is impressive, in a rather sad, resigned way, but the work ends in a fugue on one of those sewing-machine themes which occasionally turn up in Bach. All the player can do is hold the cloth steady, so to speak, and keep treadling away. Valenti does the improvisational sections rather imaginatively, as does Bundervoët among the pianists.
——Valenti, harpsichord. LYRICHORD LL 48 (see S. 913).
——Bundervoët, piano. LONDON DTL 93051 (see S. 912).
——Jambor, piano. CAPITOL PBR 8354 (see S. 906).
——Eugene Istomin, piano. COLUMBIA ML 4343 (with Violin Concerto in A minor, Piano Concerto in F minor, Trio Sonata in G, S. 1038).

FANTASY IN C MINOR, S. 919

Cöthen, about 1720. A short piece (twenty-five measures) very much like one of the two-part Inventions. Landowska plays it impeccably.

——Landowska, harpsichord. RCA VICTOR LM 1217 (with S. 972, 998; works by Scarlatti and others).

FANTASY IN G MINOR, S. 920

Not a very interesting work, consisting largely of passagework and arpeggios. Its authenticity has been questioned.

——Jambor, piano. CAPITOL PBR 8354 (*see* S. 906).

FANTASY IN A MINOR, S. 922

Weimar, about 1710. This starts out very promisingly as a clever display piece but after a while it bogs down in harmonic progressions that take a long time to reach any destination. Both pianists do well with the earlier portion and neither can be blamed for not doing more with the rest.

——Jambor, piano. CAPITOL PBR 8354 (*see* S. 906).
——Gianoli, piano. WESTMINSTER XWN 18100 (*see* S. 913).

FANTASY AND FUGUE IN A MINOR, S. 944

Cöthen, about 1720. The Fantasy is only a series of arpeggiated chords (ten measures) but the Fugue is, according to Spitta, the longest one for clavier that Bach completed. Since it consists of an uninterrupted run of rapid sixteenth notes, it is a kind of *perpetuum mobile,* but it sounds neither

dull nor too long in this neat, transparent performance.

——Friskin, piano. VANGUARD BG 543/5 (*see* S.
772-786).

SONATA IN D, S. 963

Arnstadt, 1704. A rather uncharacteristic composition, not only in its title but also in content, which
includes a simple, song-like first section and a fugue
whose theme is labeled "in imitation of a hen's
cackling." It is a lightweight work. Miss Slenczynska plays it in her customary clean but slightly
romanticizing manner.

——Slenczynska, piano. MUSIC LIBRARY MLR 7030
(*see* S. 903).

ITALIAN CONCERTO, S. 971

Published 1735. Landowska follows the printed text
strictly here. She has the advantage over the pianists of being able to differentiate, by registration,
between solo and tutti passages. Her slow movement is an object lesson in obtaining a nuanced
and flexible melodic line on the harpsichord, which
isn't supposed to permit any such thing. The piano
versions are all good, and the order in which they
are listed is not intended as a judgment of relative
value. There are differences, of course. Serkin's slow
movement, for example, is poetic and restrained;
Slenczynska's tends toward the romantic, with typical piano colors—it is not, however, overdone; Jambor, Friskin, and Wollmann are somewhat less
eloquent. On the other hand, Serkin's fast movements seem a little faster than they need be,

Friskin's a little slower, while the others are convincing. Wollmann's tone hardens in *forte*.

——Landowska, harpsichord. RCA VICTOR LCT 1137 (*see* S. 825).

——Serkin, piano. COLUMBIA ML 4350 (*see* S. 903).

——Slenczynska, piano. MUSIC LIBRARY MLR 7030 (*see* S. 903).

——Jambor, piano. CAPITOL P 8348 (*see* S. 894).

——Friskin, piano. VANGUARD BG 543/5 (*see* S. 772-786).

——Wollmann, piano. WESTMINSTER 18105 (*see* S. 831).

CONCERTOS (6) AFTER VIVALDI, S. 972-973, 975-976, 978, 980

Weimar, 1708-1717. Bach arranged for solo clavier some sixteen concertos, mostly for violin, by Italian and German composers. Of these, six have been identified as works by Vivaldi—three from Op. 3, two from Op. 4, and one from Op. 7. There is an occasional eloquence and largeness of conception in the performances by Señora Goldschwartz that recall her teacher, Landowska, but those qualities are present in the playing of Miss Marlowe too, together with a clearer differentiation between tutti and solo passages. If only one of these works is desired, one could hardly select a better one than the jolly Concerto in D, S. 972, in the superlative performance by Landowska. On the review copy of the McIntosh disk the labels are transposed.

——Marlowe, harpsichord. CAPITOL P 8361.

——(S. 976, 978, 980 only) Julieta Goldschwartz, harpsichord. McINTOSH MC 1001 (with S. 974).

——(S. 972 only) Landowska, harpsichord. RCA
VICTOR LM 1217 (*see* S. 919).

CONCERTO AFTER MARCELLO, IN D MINOR, S. 974

Based on a noble oboe concerto attributed to Bene-
detto Marcello but more probably by his brother
Alessandro. It is acceptably performed.
——Goldschwartz, harpsichord. MCINTOSH MC 1001
(*see* S. 972).

ARIA WITH THIRTY VARIATIONS (GOLDBERG VARI-ATIONS), S. 988

Published 1742. This remarkable set is not concerned with the melody of the Sarabande that
serves as "aria"; it is a group of fantastically varied
structures over the bass line that accompanies the
aria. Landowska is not overwhelming here, as she
is in the Chromatic Fantasy, but her performance
is still, in my opinion, superior to the others in
authority, depth of insight, and sheer virtuosity. She
repeats the first (or last) eight measures after the
end of some of the variations (Nos. 5, 7, 18) as
though she were loath to quit them so soon; less
acceptable are a few bits of unconvincing rubato. In
comparison Leonhardt is very correct but not very
imaginative. Some of his variations are a shade
slower than they need be, and metronomic; others
lack the grace that Landowska shows us they can
have. More interesting, even though it employs a
piano, is Gould's highly sensitive and polished performance. While some of his tempos seem a bit
fast, his playing as a whole is equaled only by
Landowska's in eloquence. Demus' is the liveliest
of his Bach performances on records. Both Friskin

and Jones play neatly but otherwise with no particular distinction.

——Landowska, harpsichord. RCA VICTOR LM 1080.

——Glenn Gould, piano. COLUMBIA ML 5060.

——Demus, piano. WESTMINSTER XWN 18227.

——Gustav Leonhardt, harpsichord. VANGUARD BG 536.

——William Corbett Jones, piano. MUSIC LIBRARY MLR 7073.

——Friskin, piano. VANGUARD BG 558.

ARIA VARIATA ALLA MANIERA ITALIANA, IN A MINOR, S. 989

This rather early work (Weimar, about 1709) consists of ten variations on a highly embellished theme. Although they are not in the same class as the "Goldberg" Variations, they are by no means lacking in interest. Gerlin's performance is excellent, the Wollmann is acceptable.

——Ruggero Gerlin, harpsichord. OISEAU-LYRE OL 50097 (with S. App. 86; works by C.P.E., W. F. Bach).

——Wollmann, piano. WESTMINSTER XWN 18105 (*see* S. 831).

CAPRICCIO ON THE DEPARTURE OF HIS BELOVED BROTHER, S. 992

Arnstadt, 1704. This charming little piece of program music, written when Bach was nineteen, is pleasingly played by Friskin.

——Friskin, piano. VANGUARD BG 543/5 (*see* S. 772-786).

PRELUDE, FUGUE, AND ALLEGRO IN E-FLAT, S. 998

The manuscript indicates that at least the Prelude was written for lute or harpsichord. It is not, in my opinion, a particularly interesting work, but all three players perform it with enthusiasm. *See also below*, under *Lute Music*.
——Landowska, harpsichord. RCA VICTOR LM 1217 (*see* S. 919).
——Valenti, harpsichord. LYRICHORD LL 48 (*see* S. 913).
——Jambor, piano. CAPITOL P 8348 (*see* S. 894).

FANTASY IN C MINOR, S. APP. 86

Although the source in which this work has survived attributes it to J. S. Bach, it is not listed by Schmieder among the authentic works. It has a kind of pathos that seems more characteristic of the young Philipp Emanuel or of Wilhelm Friedemann than of their father. Both performances are acceptable.
——Gerlin, harpsichord. OISEAU-LYRE OL 50097 (*see* S. 989).
——Jambor, piano. CAPITOL PBR 8354 (*see* S. 906).

CHAMBER AND ORCHESTRAL WORKS

BACH did not essay any category of composition that he did not enrich. In the great choral works he attained sublimity; in some of the organ works he engaged in intimate and ecstatic prayer; the clavier works include music written for educational purposes but raised to the level of high art. The chamber and orchestral works are social music, written for the enjoyment of the players and their guests, of Bach's princely employer at Cöthen or another noble music-lover, of the members of the Collegium Musicum at Leipzig. Yet to please these people was for Bach a task hardly less exalted than the service of the Lord and of the young. For the creation of music, for whatever purpose, was to him a sacred privilege and duty, without which life was inconceivable. And for these occasional pieces he drew without stint from the bottomless well of his resources of melody and harmony and counterpoint, constantly experimenting with form and design and texture.

In the bewildering variety of works that he produced in this field we find such extremes as a grand and noble fugue for a single violin and a gay little dance for about as large an orchestra as Bach ever dealt with. And between these extremes are such masterpieces as the lovely sonatas for violin and harpsichord and flute and harpsichord, the impassioned and dramatic concertos for one or more violins or harpsichords with orchestra, and the healthy, robust, yet finely drawn "Brandenburg" Concertos. At the end of his life come the two works—the *Musical Offering* and the *Art of the Fugue*—that sum up the accumulated gains of centuries of contrapuntal writing. But the *Art of the Fugue,* especially, is music so moving that technical considerations recede into the background, and the blind old Master stands revealed once more as a tremendous creative force.

LUTE WORKS

Suite in G minor, S. 995; Suite in E minor, S. 996; Prelude and Fugue in E-flat, S. 998

Whether Bach could play the lute himself and wrote all of these pieces for it (as well as some others that are attributed to him) has been the subject of some discussion in the Bach literature. It has been pointed out that Bach owned a lute and had an expert lutenist among his pupils; and lute-players say that these works lie well for their instrument and were written by someone familiar with its technique. The G minor Suite is a transcription of the Suite No. 5 for unaccompanied cello, and the Prelude and Fugue lack the final Allegro that follows them in the Complete Edition. Neither the music nor its performance, it seems to me, lifts this disk out of its special status as an item principally for Bach specialists and lute enthusiasts. For keyboard performances of S. 998, *see above*, under *Clavier Works*.

——Michel Podolski, lute. PERIOD SPL 724.

SUITE IN C MINOR, S. 997

An attractive work, with an expressive prelude and a sarabande that begins like the last movement of the *St. Matthew Passion*. Schmieder lists it among the lute compositions; there is pretty general agreement that it is not a clavier work, which is the way it was published in the Complete Edition. There seems to be no good reason for objecting to the present arrangement, made by Veyron-Lacroix for flute and harpsichord. The bass is tastefully "realized" and the work is nicely played.

——Jean-Pierre Rampal, flute; Robert Veyron-Lacroix, harpsichord. HAYDN HSL 80 (with Vivaldi: Concerto for Flute, Oboe, Violin, Bassoon, and Figured Bass, in G minor; Sonata for Flute and Figured Bass, in D minor).

PRELUDE IN C MINOR, S. 999; FUGUE IN G MINOR, S. 1000

The Prelude is one of Bach's atmospheric little pieces and the Fugue is a transcription for lute of the second movement of the G minor Sonata for unaccompanied violin. Segovia plays them with his customary musicality. His virtuosity in the Fugue is remarkable. Also included on these disks are two movements from the Lute Suite in E minor, S. 996.

——Andrés Segovia, guitar. 10-in. M-G-M E 123

(with four other pieces and transcriptions). Also 12-in. M-G-M E 3015 (with same pieces and three preludes and fugues for organ).

CHAMBER MUSIC

SONATAS AND PARTITAS FOR UNACCOMPANIED VIO-
LIN, S. 1001-1006, COMPLETE

These six compositions are one of the glories of the violin literature and the despair of countless violin-ists. To play them properly requires deep insight into a type of musical structure that does not yield its secrets easily, a lively but controlled tempera-ment, and a technique that overcomes all obstacles. The combination of these qualities in a single player is, obviously, rare; and none of the perform-ances dealt with here is so convincing as to compel one to exclaim, "This is it!" Nevertheless all of them have value or interest for one reason or another, and some of the readings of single works are as good as we are likely to get in a world where fiddlers are only human.

The three sonatas each consist of four movements in the pattern slow-fugue-slow-fast. In each case the second slow movement is in a key different from but related to that of the other sections of the work. The partitas contain five or more movements, almost all being in the idealized dance forms of the time. Here the same key is maintained throughout each work. In other words, the sonatas correspond to the "church sonatas" of the Italian baroque, while the partitas correspond to the "chamber sonatas."

Some years ago there arose a movement advocating the return to a curved bow in playing these works. It was claimed that the chords in these compositions were meant to be played solid, not arpeggiated as they must be if a modern bow and bridge are used. There is strong evidence to contradict this view, but that did not deter members of the movement from experimenting with curved bows and flatter bridges. The Schroeder set represents the results of one such experiment. It is not, it seems to me, a success. The tone is thin, spread, and wiry; despite the curved bow, some of the multiple stops sound awkward and coarse; and the musical interpretation is not exactly inspired. Another experiment —this one more successful—is offered in the Telmanyi set. His bow, while curved, is fitted with a new gadget which enables him to control the tension of the hairs at will. His tone is much pleasanter than Schroeder's, and the chords sound rich and sonorous. The playing in general, however—probably owing to the relative unfamiliarity of the bow —is not very lively. Moreover, it makes everything sound too easy; the vicarious thrills we get in following a performance on the modern instrument are diluted.

Such thrills are present in abundance in the Heifetz and Milstein sets. Milstein does not quite match his colleague in bravura, though he can play with plenty of dash when he feels like it. He is, however, much more faithfully recorded. The Martzy, too, is distinguished for superior beauty of tone and clarity of recording, but is not so strong musically.

——Jascha Heifetz, violin. Three 12-in. RCA VICTOR LM 6105.

——Nathan Milstein, violin. Three 12-in. CAPITOL PCR 8370.

——Johanna Martzy, violin. Three 12-in. ANGEL 35280/82.

——Emil Telmanyi, using the "Vega" Bach Bow. Three 12-in. LONDON LLA 20.

——Ralph Schroeder, using a curved bow. Three 12-in. COLUMBIA SL 189.

SONATA NO. 1, IN G MINOR, S. 1001

From the standpoint of sheer violin-playing, every one of the first seven recordings listed below has a good deal to be said for it. None of them, however, reveals any great depth of insight into the structure of the music. All in all, Heifetz and Milstein seem to come off best, with Ricci and Olevsky next. Martzy has a lovely tone but could do with more bravura in the Fugue and more rhythmic vitality in the Siciliano. Oistrakh, son of the celebrated David, plays quite acceptably on the whole, but the reproduction here is not as lifelike as in the other disks.

——Heifetz, in RCA VICTOR LM 6105.

——Milstein, in CAPITOL PCR 8370 or on P 8298 (with Partita No. 2).

——Ruggiero Ricci. LONDON LL 1706 (with Partita No. 2).

——Julian Olevsky. WESTMINSTER XWN 18023 (with Partita No. 2).

——Martzy, on ANGEL 35280.

——Igor Oistrakh, COLOSSEUM CRLP 193 (with Sonata No. 5, in F minor, for violin and piano; Vitali: Chaconne).

——Telmanyi, in LONDON LLA 20.
——Schroeder, in COLUMBIA SL 189.

SONATA NO. 2, IN A MINOR, S. 1003

Both the Olevsky and Martzy performances are respectable though not exciting. While Olevsky's *Grave* has a moving quality, neither he nor the dulcet-toned Miss Martzy has the technical aplomb of Heifetz or the bravura with which that wizard sweeps through the fast movements.

——Heifetz, in RCA VICTOR LM 6105.
——Milstein, in CAPITOL PCR 8370.
——Olevsky, on WESTMINSTER WN 18072 (with Partita No. 3).
——Martzy, on ANGEL 35281.
——Telmanyi, in LONDON LLA 20.
——Schroeder, in COLUMBIA SL 189.

PARTITA NO. 2, IN D MINOR, S. 1004

The crown of this work, and indeed of the whole set, is of course the giant Chaconne, which has been subjected to all kinds of mayhem in the form of transcriptions for anything from a guitar to a symphony orchestra. Here all of our violinists put their best foot forward, and it is even more difficult than usual to choose among them. The order of the listing below should not be taken too seriously. The greatest intensity is to be found in Heifetz and Francescatti. Milstein's performance, while somewhat more detached, is also first-rate; and Olevsky, Ricci, and Martzy are close behind. Francescatti makes his points a little more obviously than the others. Heifetz, Francescatti, and Milstein all indulge in a bit of rhythmical shenanigans—Heifetz and Milstein in the third variation from the end, and Heifetz and Francescatti in the next variation. The others all stick to the score, as do these men everywhere else.

——Heifetz, in RCA Victor lm 6105.

——Milstein, in Capitol pcr 8370 or on p 8298 (with Sonata No. 1).

——Zino Francescatti, violin. Columbia ml 4935 (with Partita No. 3).

——Ricci, on London ll 1706 (with Sonata No. 1).

——Martzy, on Angel 35281.

——Olevsky, on Westminster xwn 18023 (with Sonata No. 1).

——Telmanyi, in London lla 20.

——Schroeder, in Columbia sl 189.

Sonata No. 3, in C, S. 1005 (5 Editions)

Heifetz here, too, though Milstein and Martzy are almost as distinguished.

——Heifetz, in RCA Victor lm 6105.

——Milstein, in Capitol pcr 8370.

——Martzy, on Angel 35282.

——Michael Rabin, violin. Angel 35305 (with Ÿsaye: Sonatas Nos. 3 and 4).

——Telmanyi, in London lla 20.

——Schroeder, in Columbia sl 189.

Partita No. 3, in E, S. 1006

A toss-up among the first five listed below. Martzy has the most appealing tone. Sound first-rate in Capitol, Columbia, Westminster, and Angel, with the Victor only a step below.

——Milstein, in Capitol pcr 8370.

——Olevsky, on Westminster wn 18072 (with Sonata No. 2).

——Francescatti, on Columbia ml 4935 (with Partita No. 2).

——Martzy, on Angel 35282.

——Heifetz, in RCA Victor lm 6105.

——Telmanyi, in London lla 20.

——Schroeder, in Columbia sl 189.

Suites for Unaccompanied Cello, S. 1007-1012, Complete

These suites are not, in my opinion, among Bach's great works. Aside from one or two movements that have achieved a measure of popularity (but in piano arrangements), they offer little to delight the ear or stir the viscera. For the cellist's practice-room and the scholar's study they are of course important, but for sheer listening pleasure they seem to me among the least enjoyable of Bach's works. This, I gather, is not an opinion that is shared by Janigro. He lavishes upon these dry and elephantine compositions the resources of an excellent technique and a good tone. In some of the preludes he even manages to achieve some eloquence. The recording is so clear that one occasionally hears the cellist's breathing. In the second and sixth suites (xwn 18350) no visible bands separate the movements; and in the reviewer's copy there is a defective groove in the Allemande of No. 6.

On the Decca disks the suites are played skillfully and with a beautiful tone on the viola. Miss Fuchs makes rather free with the rhythm in some of the movements, but one can hardly blame her for attempting to avoid a metronomic beat and to lend interest to the phrasing.

——Antonio Janigro, cello. Three 12-in. Westminster xwn 18349, 18350, 18073.

——Lillian Fuchs, viola. Three 12-in. DECCA DL 9544, 9660, 9914.

SUITE No. 1, IN G, S. 1007

——Janigro, on WESTMINSTER XWN 18349.
——Fuchs, on DECCA DL 9914.
[——Janos Starker, cello. PERIOD 582 (with Suite No. 4).]

SUITE No. 2, IN D MINOR, S. 1008

If these suites must be played in public, then Casals' is the way to play them. His penetrating musicianship and infectious verve are combined here in a performance that is a model in every respect but one—his rather cavalier treatment of the letter of the text. In one measure of the Praeludium he changes the notes; in the Allemande he adds some as bass; in the Sarabande he omits one. No doubt he has thought long and hard about these things in a lifetime of study, but knowing his reverence for Bach one finds such changes puzzling. The recording is old but still acceptable. Janigro and Rostropovich are more faithful to the text, and more reserved in their interpretation of it.

——Pablo Casals, cello. RCA VICTOR LCT 1104 (with Suite No. 3).
——Janigro, on WESTMINSTER XWN 18350.
——Mstislav Rostropovich, cello. VANGUARD VRS 6026 (with Suite No. 5 and two transcriptions).
——Fuchs, on DECCA DL 9544.

SUITE No. 3, IN C, S. 1009

Mainardi turns in a clean, straightforward job, but even though he is favored with better recording than Casals, he is no match for his illustrious competitor. Both players take a few liberties with the text in the Gigue, Mainardi's being even less excusable than Casals'.

——Casals, RCA Victor lct 1104 (with Suite No. 2).

——Janigro, on Westminster xwn 18349.

——Enrico Mainardi, cello. 10-in. London lps 403.

——Fuchs, on Decca dl 9914.

[——Janos Starker, cello. Period 543 (with Suite No. 6).]

Suite No. 4, in E-flat, S. 1010

A particularly dreary Praeludium and a relatively gay Bourrée are features of this Suite, which is well enough played by Mainardi. One wonders why it should take both sides of a twelve-inch disk when Janigro, with not very different tempos, gets it onto one side.

——Janigro, on Westminster wn 18073.

——Mainardi. London llp 404.

——Fuchs, on Decca dl 9660.

[——Starker. Period 582 (with Suite No. 1).]

Suite No. 5, in C minor, S. 1011

——Janigro, on Westminster wn 18073.

——Rostropovich, on Vanguard vrs 6026.

——Fuchs, on Decca dl 9660.

Suite No. 6, in D, S. 1012

——Janigro, on Westminster xwn 18350.

——Fuchs, on Decca dl 9544.

[——Starker. Period 543 (with Suite No. 3).]

SONATA IN A MINOR FOR UNACCOMPANIED FLUTE,
S. 1013 (*See* Sonatas for Flute and Clavier,
S. 1030-1035)

SONATAS FOR VIOLIN AND CLAVIER, S. 1014-1019,
COMPLETE

These six sonatas are among the cream of Bach's chamber music. All of them have the clear-cut themes, the variety of moods, the extraordinary harmonic ingenuity, and the unsurpassable contrapuntal skill characteristic of their composer. Most of the slow movements are very beautiful (the Largo of No. 5 is a particularly outstanding example), and most of the fast ones have an incisiveness and a communicative power that raise them above the status of merely skillfully wrought sound patterns. The theme of the first Allegro of No. 3 has such a catchy, folk-like character that it is surprising that the Tin Pan Alley boys haven't done anything with it yet. Each of the first five sonatas is in four sections, in the order slow-fast-slow-fast. The sixth is the maverick of the group: it is in five sections; the key scheme does not follow the pattern that is pretty consistently observed in the others; and the work is the only one of the six that has a movement for clavier solo. Bach tinkered with this sonata twice after its first version was finished.

It is regrettable that no satisfactory recording of the set is now available. The harpsichord is much to be preferred to the piano here. Not only does its tone harmonize better with that of the fiddle, but it has the required rhythmic precision and, because of its coupler mechanism, a brightness of timbre that the piano lacks. One has only to compare the

Landowska recording of No. 3 (*see below*) with the same work in the present set to see how pale, relatively, the piano is. The performances here are clean and pleasant, if not particularly exciting. There is an excellent balance between violin and piano. Menuhin does not penetrate very far below the surface, but he manages to achieve an attractive tone without too much vibrato.

——Yehudi Menuhin, violin; Louis Kentner, piano. Two 12-in. RCA VICTOR LHMV 1016/17.

SONATA No. 3, IN E, S. 1016

Both the Columbia and the earlier Victor are excellent performances. The Menuhin-Landowska still sounds good, despite its age, even though the right-hand part of the harpsichord is sometimes a bit faint. If you want the keyboard part played on a harpsichord, as Bach intended it to be, then this is for you. If you don't mind the piano and prefer a silkier violin tone, the Stern-Zakin is your disk.

——Yehudi Menuhin, violin; Wanda Landowska, harpsichord. RCA VICTOR LCT 1120 (with Concerto for Two Violins in D minor).

——Isaac Stern, violin; Alexander Zakin, piano. COLUMBIA ML 4862 (with Sonata in E minor, S. 1023; Sonata in G minor, S. 1020).

——Menuhin and Kentner, on RCA VICTOR LHMV 1016.

SONATA No. 5, IN F MINOR, S. 1018

Oistrakh's playing is lovely and somewhat more imaginative than Menuhin's, but the recorded sound is definitely inferior.

——David Oistrakh, violin; Lev Oborin, piano. 12-

in. COLOSSEUM CRLP 193 (with Sonata in G minor,
S. 1001; Vitali: Chaconne).

——Menuhin and Kentner, on RCA VICTOR LHMV
1017.

SONATA No. 6, IN G, S. 1019

The comment made in connection with S. 1018
applies here too, except that the sound of the
Oistrakh is quite good here.

——David Oistrakh, violin; Vladimir Yampolsky,
piano. MONITOR MC 2009 (with Concerto for Two
Violins in D minor; Hindemith: Sonata in E-flat,
Op. 11, No. 1; Sarasate: *Navarra*).

SONATA IN G MINOR FOR VIOLIN (OR FLUTE) AND CLAVIER, S. 1020

An agreeable work, possibly originally for flute
rather than violin, with some curiously Brahmsian
sixths in the Adagio. Its authenticity has been
questioned, but most authorities consider it an
early work by Bach. Nicely performed by all four
pairs, although the Finale seems a little too fast as
done by the French artists.

——John Wummer, flute; Fernando Valenti, harpsichord. In WESTMINSTER XWN 2215 (with Sonatas
for Flute and Harpsichord).

——Isaac Stern, violin; Alexander Zakin, piano.
COLUMBIA ML 4862 (with Sonata in E, S. 1016;
Sonata in E minor, S. 1023).

——Jean-Pierre Rampal, flute; Robert Veyron-Lacroix, harpsichord; Jean Huchot, cello. LONDON DTL
93058 (with S. 1033-35).

——Louis Speyer, oboe; Daniel Pinkham, harpsichord. UNICORN UNLP 1028 (with sonatas by Hindemith and Dutilleux).

SONATA IN G FOR VIOLIN AND CLAVIER, S. 1021

This sonata, the discovery of which was announced in 1928, is for violin and figured bass and is played here by violin, harpsichord, and cello. Both the work and its performance are pleasant, if not particularly inspired.
——Ulrich Grehling, violin; Irmgard Lechner, harpsichord; Martin Bochmann, cello. OISEAU-LYRE OL 50015 (with Sonata in G, S. 1038; Sonata in E minor, S. 1034; Trio in D minor, S. 1036).

SONATA IN E MINOR FOR VIOLIN AND CLAVIER, S. 1023

This sonata (labeled "partita" on the Columbia disk), for violin and figured bass, consists of a rhapsodic introduction, a fine adagio, an only moderately interesting allemande, and a characteristic gigue. The editor of Stern's version is not named; Rostal uses an edition by Howard Ferguson. Rostal, supported by the more authentic accompanying apparatus, plays with a quite un-Bachian vibrato in the slow movement. There is more fire and less schmalz in the performance by Stern.
——Isaac Stern, violin; Alexander Zakin, piano. COLUMBIA ML 4862 (with Sonata in E, S. 1016; Sonata in G minor, S. 1020).
——Max Rostal, violin; Frank Pelleg, harpsichord; Antonio Tusa, cello. CONCERT HALL CHS 1174 (with Biber: Passacaglia; Tartini: Violin Concerto in G minor).

SONATAS FOR VIOLA DA GAMBA AND CLAVIER, S. 1027-1029, COMPLETE

The first of these sonatas, in G major, is an especially attractive work, but the other two seem less interesting, for all their good tunes and impeccable workmanship. Both Wenzinger and Scholz play them very capably. Scholz's tempos in the fast movements are perhaps a little brisker but in some passages his gamba, leading for the moment, is covered up by the harpsichord. This ticklish problem of balance is better solved in the Wenzinger recording. To modern ears the tone of a cello—especially in the hands of a Casals—is more expressive than that of a gamba, but the Columbia recording is another proof that the piano is not often a satisfactory substitute for the harpsichord in baroque ensemble music. The engineers favored the cello here, and the piano sounds a little distant; but even if the balance had been better, Bach's lines would still be blurred on that instrument as played here compared to the sharp, rhythmic crispness of the harpsichord. Some faulty grooves near the end of the first movement of No. 3 on the Vox review disk.

——August Wenzinger, viola da gamba; Fritz Neumeyer, harpsichord. ARCHIVE ARC 3009.

——Janos Scholz, viola da gamba; Egida Giordani Sartori, harpsichord. VOX PL 9010.

——Pablo Casals, cello; Paul Baumgartner, piano. Two 12-in. COLUMBIA ML 4349/50 (with Chromatic Fantasy and Fugue and Italian Concerto on latter).

SONATA NO. 1, IN G, S. 1027

Fournier's playing here is often fine-grained and elegant, and the balance between cello and piano is better than in the Casals. Since the music goes below the lowest open string of the ordinary viola only once, Vardi is enabled to play it on that instrument without shifting registers except for that one time. He is a skillful violist with a fine tone, but this music does not seem to have stirred his imagination.

——Wenzinger, on ARCHIVE ARC 3009.

——Scholz, on VOX PL 9010.

——Pierre Fournier, cello; Ernest Lush, piano. LONDON LL 700 (with short pieces by Bach, Bloch, Kreisler, Debussy, Fauré, Gershwin, Nin).

——Casals, on COLUMBIA ML 4349.

——Emanuel Vardi, viola; Vivian Rivkin, piano. 10-in. REGENT MG 5003 (with Sonata No. 2).

SONATA NO. 2, IN D, S. 1028

Good balance and fine tone in the clean and straightforward performance by Piatigorsky and Berkowitz. There are times when the ornament for a particular figure is played by one artist and not the other, an inconsistency that does not seem justified by the results. Vardi's playing is just as skillful and as unimaginative here as in No. 1; and this time he shifts an octave higher even when he doesn't have to, a procedure that plays hob with Bach's carefully calculated layout.

——Wenzinger, on ARCHIVE ARC 3009.

——Scholz, on VOX PL 9010.

——Gregor Piatigorsky, cello; Ralph Berkowitz,

piano. RCA Victor lm 1792 (with Prokofiev: Sonata for Cello and Piano, in C, Op. 119).
——Casals, on Columbia ml 4349.
——Emanuel Vardi, viola; Vivian Rivkin, piano. 10-in. Regent mg 5003 (with Sonata No. 1).

Sonatas for Flute and Clavier, S. 1030-1035

All six performers are artists, but the Westminster set seems superior for several reasons. Some of the tempos employed by Wummer seem better chosen: the first movement of the first sonata and the last movement of the third, for example, sound hurried in the Decca set, as does the Finale of S. 1033 in the London. The recording in the Decca is "close-to," with the result that while Baker's full, round tone is done justice to, Miss Marlowe's harpsichord sounds blurry compared with the clean incisiveness of Valenti's instrument, particularly with respect to the right-hand part. In the London, the flute is favored slightly on one of the sides, and on another there is a bit of extraneous noise. A point in favor of the London is the interesting realization of the figured bass in S. 1033-1035. Wummer and Baker omit the first movement of the A major Sonata, which is incomplete in Bach's manuscript. The Westminster and London sets contain, in addition to the six works represented in the Decca, a Sonata in G minor (S. 1020, *see above*) and Sonata in A minor for Unaccompanied Flute, S. 1013.

The authenticity of these last two as well as of two of the other six (S. 1031 and 1033) has been questioned (contrary to the statement in the Westminster notes, which are unusually poor in several respects). But at least four of the sonatas are undeniably by Bach; and their lovely material and delicate workmanship place them among his most attractive chamber-music compositions.

——John Wummer, flute; Fernando Valenti, harpsichord. Two 12-in. WESTMINSTER XWN 2215, or XWN 18351/52.

——Jean-Pierre Rampal, flute; Robert Veyron-Lacroix, harpsichord; Jean Huchot, cello. LONDON DTL 93058 and (without Huchot) 93107.

——Julius Baker, flute; Sylvia Marlowe, harpsichord. Two 12-in. DECCA DX 113.

SONATA IN E MINOR, S. 1034

Both the London and the Oiseau-Lyre are well-played performances whose excellence is enhanced by the addition of a cello, customary in Bach's time.

——Rampal, Veyron-Lacroix, and Huchot, on LONDON DTL 93058.

——Kurt Redel, flute; Irmgard Lechner, harpsichord; Martin Bochmann, cello. OISEAU-LYRE 50015 (with Sonata in G, S. 1038; Sonata in G, S. 1021; Trio in D minor, S. 1036).

——Wummer and Valenti, in WESTMINSTER XWN 2215 or on XWN 18352.

——Baker and Marlowe, in DECCA DX 113.

TRIO IN D MINOR FOR FLUTE, OBOE, AND CLAVIER, S. 1036

Originally written for two violins and clavier, this work may not be by Bach at all. It has two expressive slow movements and two sprightly fast ones. Good performance.

——Kurt Redel, flute; Helmut Winschermann, oboe; Irmgard Lechner, harpsichord. OISEAU-LYRE

OL 50015 (with Sonata in G, S. 1038; Sonata in E minor, S. 1034; Sonata in G, S. 1021).

SONATA IN C FOR TWO VIOLINS AND FIGURED BASS, S. 1037

An attractive work that may not be by Bach (in some sources it is attributed to Goldberg—he of the celebrated variations). It is nicely played in all three versions. The slight wavering and hum heard in the Colosseum recording are not present in the Monitor.

——David and Igor Oistrakh, violins; Hans Pischner, harpsichord. Decca DL 9950 (with S. 1043; Tartini: Trio Sonata in F; Vivaldi: Concerto in A minor, Op. 3, No. 8).

——David and Igor Oistrakh, violins; Vladimir Yampolsky, piano. MONITOR MC 2005 (with Mozart: Violin Sonata in B-flat, K. 454; Beethoven Piano Trio in E-flat) or COLOSSEUM CRLP 246 (with Mozart: Violin Concerto in D, K. 218).

SONATA IN G FOR FLUTE, VIOLIN, AND CLAVIER, S. 1038

This trio is built throughout upon the same figured bass as the sonata in the same key for violin and continuo, S. 1021. It has been suggested that the present work may be the product of one or more of Bach's Leipzig pupils, attempting to fashion a new work on a foundation taken from one of the master's compositions. The attempt, I should say, was successful. In any case, the comparison between two works with the same bass but almost entirely different superstructures is interesting and instructive. The Oiseau-Lyre performance is competent, employs a harpsichord, and was recorded with more "presence"; the Columbia recording is still adequate, uses a piano, and the players are excellent. My own tendency would be to lean toward the slightly less elegant playing of the Oiseau-Lyre because of its harpsichord and better sound.

——Kurt Redel, flute; Ulrich Grehling, violin; Irmgard Lechner, harpsichord. OISEAU-LYRE OL 50015 (with Sonata in E minor, S. 1034; Sonata in G, S. 1021; Trio in D minor, S. 1036).

——John Wummer, flute; Isaac Stern, violin; Eugene Istomin, piano. COLUMBIA ML 4353 (with Violin Concerto in A minor; Harpsichord Concerto in F minor; Toccata and Fugue in E minor).

CONCERTOS

CONCERTO FOR VIOLIN AND STRINGS, IN A MINOR, S. 1041

Barylli's playing has a relaxed and easy flow. Either because of the conception or because of the position of the microphone, the solo instrument is not very assertive; and the effect is of an orchestral concerto with occasional solos for one of the instruments. The highs are a bit strong here. The Heifetz has livelier tempos and more tension. The Old Maestro is here at the top of his form and in that happy condition he is still unbeatable. Stern, in the earlier Columbia disk, plays beautifully too, and his Andante is particularly poetic; but its effect is diluted by the heaviness with which Casals stresses the strong beats of the *ostinato* figure. Stern himself tends, in the first movement, to add emphasis to notes that are prominent anyway. These defects largely disappear in the performance with Ormandy; but here there is no continuo instrument, and it is missed especially in the first movement, which contains a number of passages where nothing is heard between the violin and the basses. The Milstein, too, suffers from the absence of a continuo, but otherwise his performance, with its warm tone and impeccable technique, is quite satisfactory. Grumiaux's conception is broad but at the same time careful about details. There is a little too much vibrato in the slow movement, and the sound is a little too brilliant. The Barchet is acceptable, despite slowish tempos and slightly over-accented highs; to me this soloist's tone is not so attractive as that of the others. Bernstein plays neatly, but there is some surface noise; and the lack of a keyboard instrument here too, as well as too much diffidence on the part of the upper orchestral strings, results in frequent gaps between top and bottom. Erlih's slow movement is sentimental.

——Jascha Heifetz, violin; Los Angeles Philharmonic Orchestra, Alfred Wallenstein, cond. RCA VICTOR LM 1818 (with Violin Concerto in E).

——Arthur Grumiaux, violin; Guller Chamber Orchestra. EPIC LC 3342 (with Violin Concerto in E).

——Nathan Milstein, violin; Festival Orchestra, Harry Blech, cond. CAPITOL P 8362 (with Mozart: Violin Concerto in A, K. 219).

——Isaac Stern, violin; Philadelphia Orchestra, Eugene Ormandy, cond. COLUMBIA ML 5087 (with

Violin Concerto in E; Vivaldi: Concerto for Two Violins in A minor).

——Isaac Stern, violin; Prades Festival Orchestra, Pablo Casals, cond. COLUMBIA ML 4353 (with Toccata and Fugue in E minor; Harpsichord Concerto in F minor; Trio Sonata, S. 1038).

——Reinhold Barchet, violin; Pro Musica String Orchestra (Stuttgart), Walther Davisson, cond. VOX PL 9150 (with Violin Concerto in E; Concerto for Two Violins in D minor).

——Walter Barylli, violin; Vienna State Opera Orchestra, Hermann Scherchen, cond. WESTMIN-STER XWN 18021 (with Violin Concerto in E).

——Joseph Bernstein, violin; Concert Hall String Ensemble. CONCERT HALL CHC 40 (with Vivaldi: Violin Concerto in A minor; Violin Sonata in A).

——Devy Erlih, violin; Pro Arte Chamber Orchestra (Munich), Kurt Redel, cond. LONDON DTL 93067 (with Violin Concerto in E; Concerto in D minor, for Two Violins).

CONCERTO FOR VIOLIN AND STRINGS, IN E, S. 1042

Several excellent performances of this fine concerto, with its unusually interesting adumbration of symphonic working-out in the first Allegro and its brooding and poetic slow movement. Only the Stevens has difficulty getting off the ground, and its sound is not so smooth as that of the others. The remarks made above concerning Heifetz, Barchet, and Barylli, in connection with the A minor Concerto, are also applicable here. As far as beauty of tone is concerned, Francescatti, Goldberg, and Kogan are here in a class with Heifetz.

But there is a tinge of nervousness in Francescatti's playing of some of the rapid figures in the first movement, the Goldberg disk contains distortion in loud passages, and the Kogan accompaniment lacks a continuo. Grumiaux's Finale seems rather slow. David Oistrakh's playing is oversweet in the slow movement and here too one misses the continuo. His son pours even more sugar into the Adagio and races through the fast movements. There is no distinction of any sort in the Merckel.

——Jascha Heifetz, violin; Los Angeles Philharmonic Orchestra, Alfred Wallenstein, cond. RCA VICTOR LM 1818 (with Violin Concerto in A minor).

——Zino Francescatti, violin; Columbia Symphony Orchestra, George Szell, cond. COLUMBIA ML 4648 (with Prokofiev: Violin Concerto No. 2).

——Szymon Goldberg, violin; Philharmonia Orchestra, Walter Susskind, cond. 10-in. DECCA DL 7507.

——Arthur Grumiaux, violin; Gullar Chamber Orchestra. EPIC LC 3342 (with Violin Concerto in A minor).

——Reinhold Barchet, violin; Pro Musica String Orchestra (Stuttgart), Walther Davisson, cond. VOX PL 9150 (with Violin Concerto in A minor; Concerto for Two Violins in D minor).

——Walter Barylli, violin; Vienna State Opera Orchestra, Hermann Scherchen, cond. WESTMINSTER WL 5318 (with Violin Concerto in A minor).

——Leonid Kogan, violin; Philharmonia String Orchestra, Otto Ackermann, cond. ANGEL 35343 (with Concerto in D minor for Two Violins; Sarabande from Partita in B minor for Unaccompanied Violin).

——David Oistrakh, violin; Philadelphia Orchestra, Eugene Ormandy, cond. COLUMBIA ML 5087 (with Violin Concerto in A minor; Vivaldi: Concerto for Two Violins in A minor).

——Henry Merckel, violin; Pro Arte Chamber Orchestra (Munich), Kurk Redel, cond. LONDON DTL 93067 (with Violin Concerto in A minor; Concerto in D minor, for Two Violins).

——Igor Oistrakh, violin; Gewandhaus Orchestra (Leipzig), Franz Konwitschny, cond. DECCA DL 9875 (with Beethoven: Romances in G and F).

——Louis Stevens, violin; Berlin Symphony Orchestra, Leopold Ludwig, cond. ROYALE 1367 (with Brandenburg Concerto No. 2).

CONCERTO FOR TWO VIOLINS AND STRINGS, IN D MINOR, S. 1043

This is one of the loveliest and most popular of all the Bach concertos. The best recorded sound may be found in Menuhin-De Vito, Gilels-Kogan, Barchet-Beh, Oistrakh, and Krebbers-Olof. The last of these may be dismissed at once, because of its sluggish tempos. The Barchet-Beh is a competent but rather unimaginative affair; the first movement is a little too comfortable and lacks excitement, while the slow movement actually drags in spots. The tone of the Oistrakhs on Monitor is oversweet, especially in the Largo, and the bass sounds tubby. This leaves the Menuhin-De Vito, which is a large-scaled conception with a broad sweep, the Oistrakhs on Decca, which is clean in the playing and in the sound, and the Gilels-Kogan, among whose merits is precise yet flexible teamwork. Probably the best violin playing is that offered by Stern-Schneider. There is a good deal of sensitive phrasing here, but especially in the Largo perhaps too much attention to detail, at the expense of the long line—a somewhat romantic approach. Erlih and Merckel offer a workaday performance and unreal sound. The Heifetz affair, with its too fast tempos, is of interest only as an engineering stunt. As for the old Menuhin-Enesco recording, it has a sentimental appeal because of the collaboration of the young artist with his celebrated teacher, but the sound is no longer acceptable.

——Yehudi Menuhin, Gioconda de Vito, violins; Philharmonia Orchestra, Anthony Bernard, cond. RCA Victor lhmv 16 (with Handel: Trio Sonata No. 2 in D; Vivaldi: Concerto in C, *Il Piacere*).

——Leonid Kogan, Elisabeth Gilels, violins; Philharmonia String Orchestra, Otto Ackermann, cond. Angel 35343 (with Violin Concerto in E; Sarabande from Partita in B minor for Unaccompanied Violin).

——David and Igor Oistrakh, violins; Gewandhaus Orchestra (Leipzig), Franz Konwitschny, cond. Decca DL 9950 (*see* S. 1037).

——Reinhold Barchet, Will Beh, violins; Pro Musica String Orchestra (Stuttgart), Walther Davisson, cond. Vox pl 9150 (with Violin Concertos in A minor and E).

——Isaac Stern, Alexander Schneider, violins; Prades Festival Orchestra, Pablo Casals, cond. Columbia ml 4351 (with Concerto for Violin and Oboe in C minor).

——David and Igor Oistrakh, violins; orchestra, Rudolf Barshai, cond. Monitor mc 2009 (with Sonata in G for Violin and Clavier; Hindemith: Violin Sonata in E-flat, Op. 11, No. 1; Sarasate: *Navarra*).

——Herman Krebbers, Theo Olof, violins; Hague Philharmonic Orchestra, Willem van Otterloo, cond. EPIC LC 3036 (with Beethoven: Romances in G and F).

——Devy Erlih, Henry Merckel, violins; Pro Arte Chamber Orchestra (Munich), Kurt Redel, cond. LONDON DTL 93067 (with Violin Concertos in A minor and E major).

——Jascha Heifetz (both solo parts); RCA Victor Chamber Orchestra, Franz Waxman, cond. RCA VICTOR LM 1051 (with Mozart: Violin Concerto No. 4).

——Yehudi Menuhin, Georges Enesco, violins; Orchestra, Pierre Monteux, cond. RCA VICTOR LCT 1120 (with Sonata in E).

CONCERTO FOR VIOLIN AND STRINGS, IN D MINOR

This is an attempt, by an unnamed person, to restore the violin concerto that is presumed to have been transcribed by Bach into his Harpsichord Concerto in D minor, S. 1052. It is an interesting experiment, more plausible in some sections than in others; but its interest was somewhat lessened for this listener by the heavy accents Casals sees fit to make on the first of each pair of eighth notes in the Adagio and by Szigeti's excessive vibrato in the same movement. A piano is used for the continuo.

——Joseph Szigeti, violin; Prades Festival Orchestra, Pablo Casals, cond. COLUMBIA ML 4352 (with Concerto for Clavier, Violin, and Flute in A minor).

CONCERTO FOR VIOLIN, OBOE AND STRINGS IN D MINOR (*see* Concerto for Two Harpsichords and Strings, in C minor, S. 1060)

CONCERTO FOR CLAVIER, VIOLIN, FLUTE, AND
    STRINGS, IN A MINOR, S. 1044

"The general character" of this concerto, says
Spitta, "is not so much deep or grand as cheerful,
delicate, and refined." The first and last movements
are based on the Prelude and Fugue in the same key
for clavier (S. 894) and the Adagio, for the soloists
alone, similarly derives from the slow movement
of the third Organ Sonata (S. 527). These are not
mere transcriptions but re-creations, and the result
is not a pastiche but a fine work that deserves to
be heard oftener than it is. In the Columbia version
the flute is a little too far back in the Allegro and
the orchestral sound is rather heavy, but otherwise
performance and recording are good. The sound
of the Vanguard is better, but there the harpsichord
is too weak in relation to the flute and violin.

——Mieczyslaw Horszowski, piano; Alexander
Schneider, violin; John Wummer, flute; Prades
Festival Orchestra, Pablo Casals, cond. COLUMBIA
ML 4352 (with Violin Concerto in D minor).

——Solisti di Zagreb, Antonio Janigro, cond. Bach
Guild BG 562 (with Concerto in D minor for Violin, Oboe, and Strings).

BRANDENBURG CONCERTOS, S. 1046-1051, COM-
    PLETE

There are several excellent recordings of these
splendid works, despite the difficulties involved in
capturing their sound with the proper clarity and
balance. These difficulties derive from the com-
binations of solo instruments of such different tonal
weights and powers of projection as oboes and

violino piccolo (in No. 1); trumpet, recorder, oboe, and violin (in No. 2); violin and recorders (in No. 4); and harpsichord and strings (in No. 5). Two of these sets—the Haas and the Horenstein—use the exact instrumentation called for by Bach throughout. All, as will be seen, have some trouble with balance.

Bach is best served, it seems to me, by Prohaska, Sacher, and Münchinger. There is little to choose among them. In all of them the tempos are convincing, and the conductors perform with the right blend of manliness and tenderness. The special virtues of the Prohaska set will be dealt with below. Sacher's players perform so well together that they even trill as one man. In the matter of embellishments Sacher is bolder than the other conductors: he adds many unwritten ornaments at likely places, a procedure that was very probably followed in Bach's own time. Münchinger's basses sound more resonant than Prohaska's; and there is indeed very little at which one could cavil in this set, aside from the slight changes in instrumentation. The Horenstein set is on the whole competently performed, and it includes the printed score. Haas's tempos lean toward the slow and heavy. Neel is stolid too, rather more than half the time. The Reiner set has some fine qualities and is well worth looking into if economy is a factor. The Casals performance cannot be recommended, despite excellent playing by some of the soloists. The orchestral sound is relatively coarse, and in several places one is made unpleasantly aware of this conductor's curious habit of overaccenting the strong beats.

——Chamber Orchestra of the Vienna State

Opera, Felix Prohaska, cond. Three 12-in. BACH GUILD BG 540/42.

——Chamber Orchestra of Basel, Paul Sacher, cond. Two 12-in. EPIC SC 6008.

——Stuttgart Chamber Orchestra, Karl Münchinger, cond. Two 12-in. LONDON LL 1457/58.

——Anonymous Orchestra, Jascha Horenstein, cond. Two 12-in. VOX DL 122.

——Boyd Neel Orchestra, Boyd Neel, cond. Two 12-in. UNICORN UNLP 1040/41.

——London Baroque Ensemble, Karl Haas, cond. Three 12-in. WESTMINSTER WAL 309.

——Soloists and Chamber Group, Fritz Reiner, cond. Three 12-in. COLUMBIA RL 3104/06.

——Prades Festival Orchestra, Pablo Casals, cond. Three 12-in. COLUMBIA ML 4345/47 (the last with excerpts from *Musical Offering*).

BRANDENBURG CONCERTO No. 1, S. 1046

Very good performances by Prohaska, Münchinger, Sacher, and Horenstein. Haas's Minuet is slow, and Casals' first movement heavy-footed. Neel is unimaginative. In the Prohaska the troublesome horn parts are beautifully played. Münchinger's and Horenstein's horns are almost as fine; Sacher's sound a bit muffled, Haas's not as clean and clear, and Reiner's too loud. The Sacher basses are a little thin. Münchinger, Reiner, Casals, and Neel use an ordinary violin instead of a violino piccolo.

——Prohaska, on BACH GUILD BG 540.

——Münchinger, on LONDON LL 222.

——Horenstein, in VOX DL 122.

——Sacher, on EPIC LC 3166.

——Reiner, on COLUMBIA RL 3104.

——Haas, on WESTMINSTER WL 5172.

——Casals, on Columbia ml 4345.
——Neel, on Unicorn 1040.

Brandenburg Concerto No. 2, S. 1047

The famous trumpet part is magnificently played in the Prokaska. We are not told what kind of trumpet is used there; but whatever it is, it sounds mellow and, while lacking the sharpness of the excellent trumpet in the Münchinger, blends better with the other instruments. It is handled with such virtuosity by Helmut Wobisch that we don't have to sit on the edge of our chairs and pray for the poor man. Prohaska's flute is a little faint. Sacher's trumpet part is managed well enough, though not with the superb assurance shown by Prohaska's man. The Fischer recording is also first-rate. Benda's trumpet is delicate and precise, but the flute is seldom clearly audible in the fast movements and the violin tone is harsh. In the Horenstein the trumpet is too far back and the oboe sometimes too loud, as is the trumpet in the Reiner. The fast movements sound hurried in the Casals. The "Centennial" has relatively high surface noise, and the Ludwig has rumbling basses and a trumpet that, like Haas's, plays an octave lower than it should. All but Haas and Horenstein use a flute instead of a recorder; and Casals employs a soprano saxophone instead of a trumpet.

——Prohaska, on Bach Guild bg 540.
——Münchinger, on London ls 226.
——Sacher, on Epic lc 3166.
——Philharmonia Orchestra, Edwin Fischer, cond. RCA Victor lhmv 8 (with Brandenburg Concerto No. 5).
——Horenstein, in Vox dl 122.

————Berlin Chamber Orchestra, Hans von Benda, cond. TELEFUNKEN LGX 66012 (with Brandenburg Concerto No. 5).

————Reiner, on COLUMBIA RL 3104.

————Casals, on COLUMBIA ML 4345.

————Neel, on UNICORN 1040.

————Haas, on WESTMINSTER WL 5113.

—Centennial [Boston] Symphony Orchestra [Serge Koussevitzky, cond.]. RCA CAMDEN CAL 147 (with Brandenburg Concerto No. 5).

————Berlin Symphony Orchestra, Leopold Ludwig, cond. ROYALE 1367 (with Violin Concerto in E).

BRANDENBURG CONCERTO No. 3, S. 1048

This concerto consists of two fast movements separated, in the printed score, by two slow chords. It seems obvious that the two chords are merely an indication for a cadenza to be improvised by the harpsichord player. A cadenza of reasonable length and weight would set off the two fast movements from each other properly. Only two of these recordings provide such a cadenza—the Prohaska and the Sacher. The others, with one exception, supply either a very brief one or simply the two chords. Reiner merely plays the chords, but otherwise his performance is as good as any; as are Horenstein's and Neel's also. Haas's tempos are rather slow. Perhaps the finest sound is offered on the Page disk. This is an intelligent reading, but lacks a continuo instrument. The Wøldike performance is clean and clear. The Balzer employs a large body of strings and has an impressive breadth. Unfortunately, there is some distortion in tuttis, and on the review disk the first few measures were missing and there were clicks. The sound of the "Centennial" will not please high-fidelity addicts, and the conductor has interpolated a *sinfonia* in place of the cadenza.

——Prohaska, on BACH GUILD BG 541.

——Sacher, on EPIC LC 3166.

——Münchinger, on LONDON LS 226.

——Reiner, on COLUMBIA RL 3105.

——Horenstein, in VOX DL 122.

——Chamber Orchestra of the Palace Chapel (Copenhagen), Mogens Wøldike, cond. RCA VICTOR LHMV 1048 (with Brandenburg Concertos Nos. 4 and 5).

——Neel, on UNICORN 1041.

——Haas, on WESTMINSTER WL 5174.

——New Orchestral Society of Boston, Willis Page, cond. COOK 1062 (with Bach-Bachrich: Suite for Strings; Villa-Lobos: *Bachianas Brasileiras* No. 5; Stravinsky: Concerto in D for String Orchestra).

——Casals, on COLUMBIA ML 4345.

——Berlin Symphony Orchestra, Joseph Balzer, cond. ROYALE 1438 (with Suite No. 4).

——Centennial [Boston] Symphony Orchestra, [Serge Koussevitzky, cond.]. RCA CAMDEN CAL 174 (with Brandenburg Concerto No. 4; C. P. E. Bach: Concerto for Orchestra in D).

BRANDENBURG CONCERTO No. 4, S. 1049

Only three of these performances employ the recorders called for by Bach instead of flutes. In the Prohaska they have a beautifully round and clear tone; in the Horenstein they are occasionally overwhelmed by the solo violin in the first movement; and in the Haas they sound thin and wheezy. Otherwise all of these recordings, as well as the

Münchinger and the Wøldike, are pretty much on a par. Sacher's harpsichord is too loud in spots and Reiner's rapid movements seem too fast. The sound of the "Centennial" is still acceptable in general, though there is some distortion in loud passages.

——Prohaska, on BACH GUILD BG 541.

——Horenstein, in VOX DL 122.

——Münchinger, on LONDON LL 222.

——Sacher, on EPIC LC 3167.

——Haas, on WESTMINSTER WL 5113.

——Danish State Radio Chamber Orchestra, Mogens Wøldike, cond. RCA VICTOR LHMV 1048 (with Brandenburg Concertos Nos. 3 and 5).

——Reiner, on COLUMBIA RL 3105.

——Casals, on COLUMBIA ML 4346.

——Neel, on UNICORN 1040.

——Centennial [Boston] Symphony Orchestra, [Serge Koussevitzky, cond.]. RCA CAMDEN CAL 174 (with Brandenburg Concerto No. 3; C. P. E. Bach: Concerto for Orchestra in D).

BRANDENBURG CONCERTO NO. 5, S. 1050

Several excellent performances here, but only one in which the balance is completely satisfactory—the Münchinger. In the Prohaska, the Sacher, and the Neel the flute is not always loud enough; and the right-hand part of the harpsichord does not always come through as clearly as it should in the Horenstein, the Reiner, and the Benda. The Wøldike is acceptable but not outstanding. Haas's reading is on the heavy side. The Fischer has excellent balance but there are occasional retards and *accelerandi*. Here, as in the Casals, the Foss, the Richter, and the "Centennial," a piano is employed instead of a harpsichord. The last-named is a typical virtuoso symphony orchestra performance with somewhat too fast tempos for the first and third movements. In the List version the sound is quite poor, the highs being so exaggerated that one's controls are helpless.

——Münchinger, on LONDON LL 222.

——Prohaska, on VANGUARD BG 542.

——Sacher, on EPIC LC 3167.

——Neel, on UNICORN 1041.

——Horenstein, in VOX DL 122.

——Reiner, on COLUMBIA RL 3106.

——Danish State Radio Chamber Orchestra, Mogens Wøldike, cond. RCA VICTOR LHMV 1048 (with Brandenburg Concertos Nos. 3 and 4).

——Berlin Chamber Orchestra, Hans von Benda, cond. TELEFUNKEN LGX 66012 (with Brandenburg Concerto No. 2).

——Haas, on WESTMINSTER WL 5174.

——Philharmonia Orchestra, Edwin Fischer, cond. RCA VICTOR LHMV 8 (with Brandenburg Concerto No. 2).

——Casals, on COLUMBIA ML 4346.

——Zimbler Sinfonietta, Lukas Foss, cond. UNICORN UNLP 1039 (with Clavier Concerto in D minor).

——National Philharmonic Orchestra, Kiril Kondrashin, cond. COLOSSEUM CRLP 250 (with Clavier Concerto in D minor).

——Centennial [Boston] Symphony Orchestra, [Serge Koussevitzky, cond.]. RCA CAMDEN CAL 147 (with Brandenburg Concerto No. 2).

——Berlin Symphony Orchestra, Karl List, cond. ROYALE 1372 (with Brandenburg Concerto No. 6).

BRANDENBERG CONCERTO No. 6, S. 1051

The performances here range from excellent to merely competent. The sound of the Prohaska is particularly rich and round and the next five are almost as satisfying. The Haas is rather dull and thick, the Casals coarse, and the List dry, with over-accented highs.

——Prohaska, on BACH GUILD BG 542.

——Münchinger, on LONDON LL 144.

——Sacher, on EPIC LC 3167.

——Horenstein, in VOX DL 122.

——Reiner, on COLUMBIA RL 3106.

——Neel, on UNICORN 1041.

——Haas, on WESTMINSTER WL 5172.

——Casals, on COLUMBIA ML 4347.

——Berlin Symphony Orchestra, Karl List, cond. 12-in. ROYALE 1372 (with Brandenburg Concerto No. 5).

CONCERTO FOR HARPSICHORD AND STRINGS, No. 1, IN D MINOR, S. 1052

The violin concerto of which this is presumably a transcription is not known. (*See above*, Concerto for Violin and Strings in D minor.) Some scholars believe that the model was not one of Bach's own compositions. Be that as it may, the concerto, in the form that has survived, is one of the finest of the lot, with a vigorous and passionate first movement, a brooding Adagio, and a lively finale. Bach seems to have been especially fond of it, because he used portions of it again in two sacred cantatas (Nos. 146 and 188). The Landowska is the most vital of these performances, but unfortunately the recording, made in 1938, sounds practically pre-historic. In the first five recordings listed below the fast movements have the proper combination of solidity with vivacity, and it is only in the Adagio that a lack of imagination and sensitivity is felt. In the Viderø, Marlowe, Reinhardt, and Richter versions the difficult problem of balance between a harpsichord and a body of strings has been on the whole successfully solved. Karl Richter's harpsichord, in its middle and low registers, lacks the sharp definition of the others and is instead rather hoarse and rasping. In the Elsner the sound of the harpsichord is occasionally drowned by the strings at the beginning, but the balance soon improves. The basses in this recording sometimes have a fuzzy sound.

Of the versions employing a piano, the one by Gould and the two by Foss seem to have most in their favor. The Gould is in fact as crisp, musical, and intelligent a performance on the piano as I have heard; the only flyspeck here is the romantic treatment of the orchestral passages opening and closing the Adagio. Of the two performances by Foss, the Unicorn has a somewhat fuller sound. S. Richter's sober performance attains eloquence in the slow movement, but the sound, in both editions, is distorted and tinny. An excellent performance by Jean Casadesus is weakened, it seems to me, by the tempo at which he plays the Adagio, a tempo that turns the movement into something graceful but rather superficial. Ellsasser's performance on the organ has to be put down as a valiant but unsuccessful experiment.
——Rolf Reinhardt, harpsichord; Pro Arte Chamber Orchestra (Munich), Kurt Redel, cond. Lon-

DON DTL 93097 (with Clavier Concertos in A and F minor).

——Sylvia Marlowe, harpsichord; Concert Arts Chamber Orchestra. CAPITOL P 8375 (with Haydn: Clavier Concerto in D).

——Finn Viderø, harpsichord; Orchestra of the Collegium Musicum (Copenhagen), Lavard Friisholm, cond. HAYDN HSL 92 (with Clavier Concertos Nos. 4 and 5).

——Helma Elsner, harpsichord; Pro Musica Orchestra (Stuttgart), Rolf Reinhardt, cond. VOX PL 9510 (with Clavier Concerto No. 2).

——Karl Richter, harpsichord; Ensemble of the Ansbach Bach Festival, Karl Richter, cond. LONDON LL 1445 (with Concerto in C major for Two Claviers).

——Glenn Gould, piano; Columbia Symphony Orchestra, Leonard Bernstein, cond. Columbia ML 5211 (with Beethoven: Piano Concerto No. 2).

——Lukas Foss, piano; Zimbler Sinfonietta, Lukas Foss, cond. UNICORN UNLP 1039 (with Brandenburg Concerto No. 5).

——Lukas Foss, piano; Zimbler String Sinfonietta. DECCA DL 9601 (with Clavier Concerto No. 5).

——Sviatoslav Richter, piano; State Orchestra of the U.S.S.R., Kurt Sanderling, cond. MONITOR MC 2002 (with Prokofiev: Violin Concerto No. 2).

——Sviatoslav Richter, piano; National Philharmonic Orchestra, K. Sanderling, cond. COLOSSEUM CRLP 250 (with Brandenburg Concerto No. 5).

——Jean Casadesus, piano; Paris Conservatoire Orchestra, André Vandernoot, cond. ANGEL 45003 (with Clavier Concerto No. 5; Toccata and Fugue in C minor, S. 911).

——Wanda Landowska, harpsichord; string ensemble, Eugène Bigot, cond. RCA VICTOR LM 1974 (with Two-Part Inventions).

——Richard Ellsasser, organ; Philharmonia Orchestra of Hamburg, Hans-Jurgen Walther, cond. M-G-M E 3365 (with Clavier Concerto No. 3).

CONCERTO FOR HARPSICHORD AND STRINGS, No. 2, IN E, S. 1053

A less interesting work than No. 1 but still worth an occasional hearing. Elsner's performance is robust and the recording is good, except for the sound of the basses, which is sometimes gruff.

——Helma Elsner, harpsichord; Pro Musica Orchestra (Stuttgart), Rolf Reinhardt, cond. VOX PL 9510 (with Harpsichord Concerto No. 1).

CONCERTO FOR HARPSICHORD AND STRINGS, No. 3, IN D, S. 1054

A transcription of the Violin Concerto in E (S. 1042). Both Nef and Rapf play well, but the Oiseau-Lyre orchestra sounds ponderous in the fast movements, and tutti chords are heavily punched out. The Ellsasser is an uneven struggle between organ and orchestra.

——Kurt Rapf, harpsichord; Vienna Chamber Orchestra, Rapf, cond. BACH GUILD BG 509 (with Harpsichord Concerto No. 4).

——Isabelle Nef, harpsichord; Ensemble Orchestral de L'Oiseau-Lyre, Pierre Colombo, cond. OISEAU-LYRE OL 50042 (with Harpsichord Concerto No. 5).

——Richard Ellsasser, organ; Philharmonia Orchestra of Hamburg, Hans-Jurgen Walther, cond. M-G-M E 3365 (with Clavier Concerto No. 1).

[——M. Van der Lyck, harpsichord; Ton Studio

Orchestra (Stuttgart), Michael, cond. PERIOD 547 (with Harpsichord Concerto No. 6).]

CONCERTO FOR HARPSICHORD AND STRINGS, No. 4, IN A, S. 1055

This fine work has a sunny, cheerful first movement, one of those brooding sicilianos that Bach loved to write as a slow movement, and a bright and dancing finale. All three performances are satisfactory, with the London having a slight superiority with respect to quality of sound.

——Rolf Reinhardt, harpsichord; Pro Arte Chamber Orchestra (Munich), Kurt Redel, cond. LONDON DTL 93097 (with Concertos Nos. 1 and 5).

——Finn Viderø, harpsichord; Orchestra of the Collegium Musicum (Copenhagen), Lavard Friisholm, cond. HAYDN HSL 92 (with Harpsichord Concertos Nos. 1 and 5).

——Kurt Rapf, harpsichord; Vienna Chamber Orchestra, Rapf, cond. BACH GUILD BG 509 (with Harpsichord Concerto No. 3).

CONCERTO FOR HARPSICHORD AND STRINGS, No. 5, IN F MINOR, S. 1056

A lovely work with a nobly melancholy first movement and a dramatic finale. The Nef harpsichord has a charming tone but her conductor is rather ponderous and indulges in an enormous retard at the end of the slow movement. The Reinhardt and the Viderø are nicely played and would be unreservedly recommended if the Largo were more imaginatively done. If you prefer the piano, Foss's playing is cleaner and crisper than Haskil's, but that lady has the advantage of a more eloquent orchestra, which is also more precise in the plucked chords of the Largo. Some of the better qualities of both are combined in the Casadesus. None of these recordings is ideal, but for all-around merit, including the proper performance of the ornaments, I should choose the Viderø.

——Finn Viderø, harpsichord; Orchestra of the Collegium Musicum (Copenhagen), Lavard Friisholm, cond. HAYDN HSL 92 (with Harpsichord Concertos Nos. 1 and 4).

——Rolf Reinhardt, harpsichord; Pro Arte Chamber Orchestra (Munich), Kurt Redel, cond. LONDON DTL 93097 (with Harpsichord Concertos Nos. 1 and 4).

——Isabelle Nef, harpsichord; Ensemble Orchestral de L'Oiseau-Lyre, Pierre Colombo, con. OISEAU-LYRE OL 50042 (with Harpsichord Concerto No. 3).

——Jean Casadesus, piano; Paris Conservatoire Orchestra, André Vandernoot, cond. ANGEL 45003 (with Harpsichord Concerto No. 1; Toccata and Fugue in C minor, S. 911).

——Lukas Foss, piano; Zimbler String Sinfonietta. DECCA DL 9601 (with Harpsichord Concerto No. 1).

——Clara Haskil, piano; Prades Festival Orchestra, Pablo Casals, cond. COLUMBIA ML 4353 (with Violin Concerto in A minor; Toccata and Fugue in E minor; Sonata for Violin, Piano, and Flute).

CONCERTO FOR HARPSICHORD AND STRINGS, No. 6, IN F, S. 1057

[——M. Van der Lyck, harpsichord; Ton Studio Orchestra (Stuttgart), Michael, cond. 12-in. PERIOD 547 (with Harpsichord Concerto No. 3). $4.98.]

CONCERTO FOR TWO HARPSICHORDS AND STRINGS, IN
   C MINOR, S. 1060

One of Bach's finest concertos. It has an expressive
first movement, whose principal theme, first presented by the full ensemble, ends with a charming
echo in the harpsichords; the slow movement is a
serene dialogue between the two keyboard instruments accompanied by plucked strings; and the
Finale is gay, despite the minor key. It is clearly and
briskly played on the Vox disk. This work is thought
to be a transcription by Bach of a lost earlier concerto for violin and oboe. Several attempts have
been made to reconstruct the original from the
transcription. One of these attempts is recorded on
the same side of the Vox and on the Bach Guild.
Transposed to D minor, it is a plausible version; the
transcriber mostly allots the right-hand part of Harpsichord I to the violin and the same part of Harpsichord II to the oboe. For some reason, however, he
(or the conductor) omits the continuo that Bach
would undoubtedly have required in the original
version. The soloists on the Columbia disk are both
first-class but the sound is rather dull and dry.
——Helma Elsner, Rolf Reinhardt, harpsichords;
Will Beh, violin; Friedrich Milde, oboe; Pro Musica
String Orchestra (Stuttgart), Reinhardt, cond. Vox
PL 9580 (with Concerto for Two Harpsichords in
C).
——Isaac Stern, violin; Marcel Tabuteau, oboe;
Prades Festival Orchestra, Pablo Casals, cond. Co-
LUMBIA ML 4351 (with Concerto in D minor for
Two Violins).
——Solisti di Zagreb, Antonio Janigro, cond. BACH

GUILD BG 562 (with Concerto in A minor for Flute, Violin, Clavier, and Strings).

CONCERTO FOR TWO HARPSICHORDS AND STRINGS, IN C, S. 1061

This is one harpsichord concerto that does not seem to be a transcription. The lovely slow movement and the fine fugue that serves as Finale more than make up for a first movement whose thematic material strikes this listener as emotionally neutral and in which the two claviers function as hardly more than counterpoint machines. The three harpsichord versions are on the whole excellently performed, although the Concert Hall chooses a rather breathless tempo for the first movement and the entrances of the fugue subject in the harpsichords could be clearer in the Vox. The Angel performance is rather tense and mechanical. The Victor recording dates from 1936; it is still acceptable, although in the transfer to LP, tape hiss has crept in, especially in the last two movements. The Schnabels play it competently. Surprisingly, there seems to be a slight difference of opinion between father and son about the phrasing of the fugue subject.

——Helma Elsner, Rolf Reinhardt, harpsichords; Pro Musica String Orchestra (Stuttgart), Reinhardt, cond. Vox PL 9580 (with Concerto for Two Harpsichords in C minor; Concerto for Violin and Oboe in D minor).

——Karl Richter, Eduard Müller, harpsichords; Ensemble of the Ansbach Bach Festival, Karl Richter, cond. LONDON LL 1445 (with Clavier Concerto No. 1).

——Hans Andreae, Theodor Sack, harpsichords;

Winterthur Symphony Orchestra, Clemens Dahinden, cond. CONCERT HALL CHS 1081 (with Haydn: Concerto in F for Violin and Harpsichord).
——Artur Schnabel, Karl Ulrich Schnabel, pianos; London Symphony Orchestra, Sir Adrian Boult, cond. RCA VICTOR LCT 1140 (with Mozart: Concerto in E-flat, K. 365).
——Clara Haskil, Geza Anda, pianos; Philharmonia Orchestra, Alceo Galliera, cond. ANGEL 35380 (with Mozart: Concerto in E-flat for Two Pianos, K. 365).

CONCERTO FOR TWO HARPSICHORDS AND STRINGS, IN C MINOR, S. 1062

A transcription of the great D minor Concerto for Two Violins (S. 1043). The transference is faithful, and a fascinating glimpse into Bach's workshop is afforded by the small changes he makes in order to accommodate to keyboard instruments the two solo parts originally conceived in terms of bowed strings. The orchestra part remains practically unaltered. The more familiar version is considerably the more effective one, but those interested in the transcription will find it very well performed here.
——Fin Viderø, Søren Sørensen, harpsichords; Orchestra of the Collegium Musicum (Copenhagen), Lavard Friisholm, con. HAYDN HSL 115 (with Concerto for Three Harpsichords in D minor).

CONCERTO FOR THREE HARPSICHORDS AND STRINGS, IN D MINOR, S. 1063

For ideal results in listening to this and the following concerto at home, we really should grow a third ear and require audio engineers to develop trinaural reproduction. Only thus could we do full justice to the masterly way in which Bach keeps each clavier an independent entity while yet blending all of them into a superb ensemble. In the concert hall, of course, when the three instruments are well separated, the problem does not arise; but when the sound comes out of a single speaker it is impossible to tell which is doing what, unless one is following with a score. Pending the necessary anatomical and acoustic developments, however, we shall have to be satisfied with what nature and the engineers have bestowed upon us.

Friisholm takes the first movement more crisply than Reinhardt and his last movement is gayer, though perhaps a bit too fast. The Siciliano has more character in the Reinhardt performance (it is a little too brisk in the Friisholm), even though Miss Elsner plays the short cadenza metronomically instead of like an improvisation. Throughout this version the low strings tend to lag slightly behind the harpsichords. Of these two disks, the Friisholm would seem to have a slight edge in musical value, while the Reinhardt has the definite advantage of containing an additional work. The Regent and London records are nicely done, but they use pianos and their sound is not the most faithful imaginable.

——Finn Viderø, Søren Sørensen, Eyvind Møller, harpsichords; Orchestra of the Collegium Musicum (Copenhagen), Lavard Friisholm, cond. HAYDN HSL 115 (with Concerto for Two Harpsichords in C minor).

——Helma Elsner, Rolf Reinhardt, Franzpeter Goebels, harpsichords; Pro Musica String Orchestra (Stuttgart), Reinhardt, cond. VOX PL 8670 (with Concerto for Three Harpsichords in C; Concerto for Four Harpsichords).

——Gisèle Kuhn, Georgette Astorg, Livia Rev; pianos; Orchestre du Théâtre des Champs-Elysées, Arthur Goldschmidt, cond. LONDON DTL 93053 (with Concerto in C for Three Harpsichords; Concerto for four harpsichords).

——Tanana-Nicoiayeva, Dmitri Shostakovich, Paul Serebsyakov, pianos; Berlin Radio Orchestra, Kiril Kondrashin, cond. 10-in. REGENT MG 5020 (with Handel: Concerto Grosso No. 7 in B-flat, Op. 6).

CONCERTO FOR THREE HARPSICORDS AND STRINGS, IN C, S. 1064

Whether this is an original work or a transcription of a concerto for three violins by Bach or someone else, is unknown. There is not much to choose between the Vox and Haydn Society recordings. Both are well performed. The Vox has a slight advantage in that the balance in it is somewhat better (the orchestra is more distinct in the first movement) and its performance has a little more vitality. Also, it contains three works instead of two. A disadvantage is that it has no visible separation between movements, while the other disks have such bands. The most expressive performance is the London directed by Richter, but here, unfortunately, much of the detail in the harpsichords is lost because the orchestral strings are relatively too loud. The far greater dynamic flexibility of the piano enables the Victor performers to obtain sharper contrast between *piano* and *forte* and allows them to bring out the principal lines better. In the Victor first movement, however, there are slight fluctuations in tempo; these were no doubt introduced for expressive purposes but the effect they produce is of nervousness. The sound on the London DTL disk is distorted.

——Helma Elsner, Renate Noll, Franzpeter Goebels, harpsichords; Pro Musica String Orchestra (Stuttgart), Rolf Reinhardt, cond. Vox PL 8670 (with Concerto for Three Harpsichords in D minor; Concerto for Four Harpsichords).

——Christa Fuhrmann, Bruno Seidlhofer, Erna Heiller, harpsichords; Vienna Chamber Orchestra, Anton Heiller, cond. HAYDN HSLP 1024 (with Concerto for Four Harpsichords).

——Karl Richter, Eduard Müller, Gerhard Aeschbacher, harpsichords; Ensemble of the Ansbach Bach Festival, Karl Richter, dir. LONDON LL 1446 (with Concerto for Four Harpsicords).

——Edwin Fischer, Ronald Smith, Denis Matthews, pianos; Philharmonia Orchestra, Fischer, cond. RCA VICTOR LHMV 1004 (with Mozart: Piano Concerto in C, K. 503).

——Gisèle Kuhn, Georgette Astorg, Livia Rev, pianos; Orchestre du Théâtre des Champs-Elysées, Arthur Goldschmidt, cond. LONDON DTL 93053 (with Concerto in D minor for Three Harpsichords; Concerto for Four Harpsichords).

CONCERTO FOR FOUR HARPSICHORDS AND STRINGS, IN A MINOR, S. 1065

It would have been interesting to have on the same disk the Vivaldi Concerto for Four Violins of which this is a transcription. All three of the present performances on harpsichords are acceptable. Reinhardt takes the jolly first movement more briskly than Heiller, but the latter maintains a slightly better balance between the solo instruments and the orchestra, which is occasionally too prominent in the Vox and London LL. The performance directed by Goldschmidt is tidy enough but the sound is unreal.

——Helma Elsner, Renate Noll, Franzpeter Goebels, Willy Spilling, harpsichords; Pro Musica String Orchestra (Stuttgart), Rolf Reinhardt, cond. Vox PL 8670 (with Concerto for Three Harpsichords in D minor; Concerto for Three Harpsichords in C).

——Erna Heiller, Bruno Seidlhofer, Christa Fuhrmann, Kurt Rapf, harpsichords; Vienna Chamber Orchestra, Anton Heiller, cond. HAYDN HSLP 1024 (with Concerto for Three Harpsichords in C).

——Karl Richter, Eduard Müller, Gerhard Aeschbacher, Heinrich Gurtner, harpsichords; Ensemble of the Ansbach Bach Festival, Karl Richter, dir. LONDON LL 1446 (with Concerto in C for Three Harpsichords).

——Gisèle Kuhn, Georgette Astorg, Livia Rev, Monique Mercier, pianos; Orchestre du Théâtre des Champs-Elysées, Arthur Goldschmidt, cond. LONDON DTL 93053 (with Concerto in D minor and Concerto in C for Three Harpsichords).

SUITES FOR ORCHESTRA

SUITES (OR OVERTURES), S. 1066-1069, COMPLETE

Bach is at his gayest and most charming in the dances of these suites, and most of the conductors of the complete sets do justice to those qualities as well as to the graver moods of the overtures proper. The choice, it seems to me, lies between the Prohaska and the Scherchen. In the former version there are excellent playing, clean sound, good tempos, and considerable nuance. There is also a bonus: the overtures of the Third and Fourth Suites are played twice—once (at the beginning of the Suite) with the unwritten dotted rhythms characteristic of the French style and once (at the end) as written. This experiment would have been even more interesting if Prohaska had used a string body of the size available to Bach—say six violins instead of fourteen. Scherchen's orchestra sounds like a fairly large one but it skips about lightly, the strings never overpowering the winds. The general vitality of his performances is enhanced by nuances of dynamics and phrasing that are immanent in the notes but not always brought to the ear —at least in so tasteful a fashion.

Van Beinum's orchestra, too, is a large one; his performances, with exceptions to be noted, are excellent.

Reiner's crack players produce the most beautiful sound of all, but some of his tempos and other interpretative ideas seem questionable. The Hewitt performances are bluff and hearty and not devoid of imagination, but there is more charm in the dances than can be heard on this recording. Klemperer's is an expert job and would have been quite satisfactory if the sound were more lifelike. The highs are exaggerated, and no amount of fiddling with the controls could bring a true string tone. Redel is quite faithful to the letter of the music but less so to the spirit. Both BACH GUILD and Angel supply the score of the suites.

——Vienna State Opera Orchestra, Felix Prohaska, cond. Two 12-in BACH GUILD BG 530/31.

——English Baroque Orchestra, Hermann Scherchen, cond. Two 12-in. WESTMINSTER WN 2201.

——Concertgebouw Orchestra of Amsterdam, Eduard van Beinum, cond. Two 12-in. EPIC SC 6024.

——RCA Victor Orchestra, Fritz Reiner, cond. Two 12-in. RCA VICTOR LM 6012.

——Hewitt Orchestra. Two 12-in. HAYDN HSL 90/91.

——Philharmonia Orchestra, Otto Klemperer, cond. Two 12-in. ANGEL 3536B.

——Pro Arte Chamber Orchestra (Munich), Kurt Redel, cond. Two 12-in. LONDON DTL 93073/74.

SUITE No. 1, IN C, S. 1066

The Casals and Van Beinum are performances of the big-orchestra type rather than the more authentic chamber orchestra kind. If you like that type of sound, you will doubtless enjoy the Hollanders particularly. The Berlin group is presumably smaller but also sounds full, owing probably to the engineering; the audio boys have not, however, solved the problem of attaining realistic violin tone in this one. Casals chooses to omit the Minuet, which is one of the dances marked as optional in the score. (In the other recordings nothing is omitted except an occasional repeat.) Scherchen includes the harpsichord—not prescribed—in the second Bourrée, but its use there is effective. An inner line is stressed by Klemperer in the second Gavotte, for which he can hardly be blamed, because that line has a surprisingly *Meistersinger*ish character.

——Prohaska, in BACH GUILD BG 530/531.

——Scherchen, on WESTMINSTER WN 18012.

——Amsterdam Concertgebouw Orchestra, Eduard van Beinum, cond. Epic lc 3194 (with Suite No. 2).

——Reiner, in RCA Victor lm 6012.

——Prades Festival Orchestra, Pablo Casals, cond. Columbia ml 4348 (with Suite No. 2).

——Klemperer, on Angel 35235.

——Hewitt, on Haydn hsl 90.

——Redel, on London dtl 93073.

Suite No. 2, in B minor, S. 1067

The best all-round version is the Münchinger. It has style and good sound, though not perhaps the best flutist; and it is the only one, besides the Prohaska, in which the appoggiaturas seem to be played properly. In the Van Beinum the flute is barely audible in non-solo passages and not far enough forward when it is playing alone. The flute-playing in the Redel is not immaculate. The Casals and the "Centennial" are good of their kind. Both have first-class soloists but both reveal a touch of romanticism here and there. The "Centennial" has noticeable surface noise. The Stokowski version is heavily "expressive," with Wagnerian swellings and exaggerated retards.

——André Pepin, flute; Stuttgart Chamber Orchestra, Karl Münchinger, cond. London ll 848 (with Suite No. 3).

——Prohaska, in Bach Guild bg 530/31.

——Scherchen, on Westminster wn 18012.

——Reiner, in RCA Victor lm 6012.

——Hubert Barwahser, flute; Amsterdam Concertgebouw Orchestra, Eduard van Beinum, cond. Epic lc 3194 (with Suite No. 1).

——Klemperer, on Angel 35235.

——John Wummer, flute; Prades Festival Orchestra, Pablo Casals, cond. COLUMBIA ML 4348 (with Suite No. 1).

——Hewitt, on HAYDN HSL 90.

——Redel, on LONDON DTL 93073.

——Centennial [Boston] Symphony Orchestra, [Serge Koussevitzky, cond.]. RCA CAMDEN CAL 158 (with Suite No. 3).

——Julius Baker, flute; Symphony Orchestra, Leopold Stokowski, cond. RCA VICTOR LM 1176 (with several Bach transcriptions).

SUITE No. 3, IN D, S. 1068

The Münchinger seems best here, as regards both interpretation and sound. Of special interest is the Weingartner, apparently the only example on LP of that great conductor dealing with Bach. It is, as one would expect, an authoritative performance and, as one might not expect, free of romantic notions. The sound is still mostly adequate but there is a bad splice in the Overture, the trumpets are a little uncertain on high notes and sometimes inaudible, and a continuo is lacking. The "Centennial" has more surface noise than the others and its conductor leans towards fast tempos. Here, too, the trumpets can barely be heard.

——Stuttgart Chamber Orchestra, Karl Münchinger, cond. LONDON LL 848 (with Suite No. 2).

——Prohaska, in BACH GUILD BG 530/31.

——Scherchen, on WESTMINSTER WN 18013.

——Van Beinum, in EPIC SC 6024 or on LC 3332.

——Reiner, in RCA VICTOR LM 6012.

——Klemperer, on ANGEL 35235.

——Hewitt, on HAYDN HSL 91.

——Redel, on London dtl 93074.

——Orchestre de la Société des Concerts du Conservatoire, Felix Weingartner, cond. Columbia ml 4783 (with Brahms: *Variations on a Theme by Haydn*).

——Centennial [Boston] Symphony Orchestra, [Serge Koussevitzky, cond.]. RCA Camden cal 158 (with Suite No. 2).

Suite No. 4, in D, S. 1069

Van Beinum's version would be the peer of any if his *Réjouissance* were a little jollier, a little less square. In the slow section of Balzer's Overture there is an attempt to reproduce the sharper rhythms of Baroque practice, but it is not as thorough or as convincing here as in the Prohaska version and it results in some rather ragged playing. Otherwise this performance is not outstanding and the sound is dry. Scherchen takes it upon himself to add a descending bassoon line in a portion of the Gavotte.

——Prohaska, in Bach Guild bg 530/31.

——Scherchen, on Westminster wn 18013.

——Reiner, in RCA Victor lm 6012.

——Van Beinum, in Epic sc 6024 or on lc 3332.

——Hewitt, on Haydn hsl 91.

——Klemperer, on Angel 35234.

——Redel, on London dtl 93074.

——Berlin Symphony Orchestra, Joseph Balzer, cond. Royale 1438 (with Brandenburg Concerto No. 3).

MUSIKALISCHES OPFER

MUSICAL OFFERING, S. 1079

What an endlessly fascinating composition this is! One never ceases to marvel at it, not merely because of what Bach does with the theme supplied by Frederick the Great—he stretches it, he contracts it, he stands it on its head, he works it backward, he builds a whole trio sonata around it, he subjects it to all sorts of fugal procedures—but because the result of all this contrapuntal ingenuity happens to be deeply affecting music as well. Bach indicated the instrumentation for only three of the thirteen sections. Each of the present versions uses a somewhat different instrumental layout. Another problem that has concerned musicologists is the proper order of the sections, which was not clear in the first edition. The solution this listener finds most convincing is that offered by Hans T. David in his admirable edition of the work. David places the trio sonata in the center, flanked on each side by five canons, with the three-part *ricercar* at the beginning and the six-part *ricercar* at the end. Münchinger's version follows David's suggestions about instrumentation in most respects, and the only radical departure from David's text is in the conductor's solution of the four-part puzzle canon —a solution that sounds quite plausible. This performance is live, intelligent, and musical. So is the Scherchen, which employs an edition by Roger Vuataz. Three of the canons are worked out differently here from the way in which they are presented by David; in at least one case the David seems to me better. Markevitch's orchestration is tasteful and his playing lovely, but his treatment of the general form seems questionable. Neither he nor Münchinger nor Scherchen follows David's structural layout. All three lump the three-part *ricercar* and all ten canons on one side of the disk and the trio sonata and six-part *ricercar* on the other side. Markevitch strings the canons together into a single connected movement and calls it "Theme with Variations," as though the other sections were not also variations. He also adds the three-part mirror canon to the trio sonata, thus effectively knocking the proportions of that section out of kilter. The Ghedini, orchestrated by the conductor, is an old-fashioned overblown transcription, with an opening brass fanfare, two pianos, sugary violin solos, and so on. It is about as far away from the spirit of Bach as it is possible to be while still using most of his notes.

——Stuttgart Chamber Orchestra, Karl Münchinger, cond. LONDON LL 1181.

——Camillo Wanausek, flute; F. Wachter, oboe; J. Noblinger, English horn; F. Killinger, bassoon; G. Swoboda, A. Bog, violins; A. Kreiner, viola; V. Gorlich, cello; Kurt Rapf, harpsichord; Hermann Scherchen, cond. WESTMINSTER XWN 18375.

——Orchestre National de la Radiodiffusion Française, Igor Markevitch, cond. ANGEL 45005.

——Scarlatti Orchestra di Napoli, Giorgio Ghedini, cond. COLOSSEUM CLPS 1044.

The three-part *ricercar*, in an effective performance for piano solo; the trio sonata in the instrumentation prescribed by Bach (flute, violin, and continuo); and the six-part *ricercar*, played by strings. ——J. Wummer, flute; A. Schneider, O. Pernel, violins; M. Thomas, K. Tuttle, violas; L. Terapulsky, D. Saidenberg, cellos; J. Rotenberg, bass; L. Mannes, piano. COLUMBIA ML 4347 (with Brandenburg Concerto No. 6).

DIE KUNST DER FUGE

THE ART OF THE FUGUE, S. 1080

It is astonishing to realize that this great work, which was published less than a year after Bach's death, was apparently not performed in public until 1927. True, no one knew how Bach intended it to be performed: in the manuscript it is written mostly on four staves, with no indication of what instrument or instruments are to play it, and the last fugue breaks off before it is finished. To the nineteenth century this masterpiece, which is not only the epitome of the application of the fugue principle to a single theme but profoundly moving music, was a cold, abstract affair, suitable only for purposes of study. It was only in our own time that scholars began to try to bring the printed notes to life; and so it is that each of these four versions represents a transcription by a living musician. And there are a number of other transcriptions, published but unrecorded. Not only the instrumentation but the order of the sections is unknown. Many editors have proposed many different solutions, each with some logic but none with enough to win any great number of adherents. This, too, is reflected in the present performances: no two of them use the same pattern.

All five have solid values. A choice among them will probably be largely determined by a preference for one medium over others. My own inclination is toward the Redel. To me this contrapuntal music calls for the utmost linear clarity, and this Redel (who conducts his own transcription) supplies in the fugues, using the clearly differentiated but warm and homogeneous voices of the string body, and adding oboes and bassoons occasionally in somewhat the same manner as a discreet organist would add reed stops. For the canons, however, he employs sometimes the harpsichord and sometimes an organ, a procedure which may be legitimate enough but which sounds dull and mechanical here. Moreover, unlike the others, he includes two fugues for harpsichords (No. 2 on Side 4) that are only Bach's arrangements of the preceding Fugue XIII.

Scherchen uses a transcription by Roger Vuataz for strings and woodwinds, the latter including only those with which Bach was familiar. Much of this is very fine, but Fugue IV sounds a little sleepy; VIII and IX seem somewhat overorchestrated; and the bassoon has some trouble with high notes in the Canon at the Octave.

Walcha is able to achieve some effects that are possible only on an organ and that seem legitimate and convincing here, and he keeps the voices distinct. It is perhaps just a matter of personal taste that makes me prefer the animated phrasing and subtle line-inflection impossible on the organ but attainable in a small orchestra. The Dichlers play sensitively a transcription for two pianos by Bruno Seidlhofer. The only objection to this (if you don't mind pianos in this music) is that the transcriber has added octaves above and below which sometimes weaken a melodic climax by anticipating the register in which it occurs. The same objection holds in the transcription for harpsichord made by Leonhardt. The polyphony is least clear here, the effect, for example, of Bach's occasional long-held notes being impossible to obtain on this instrument. Leonhardt, for some reason, breaks off the last fugue seven measures before Bach did. The microphone was apparently too close to the harpsichord in this recording. The Dichler, incidentally, is the only version that includes the chorale that was appended to the work after Bach's death.

——Orchestre de Chambre Pro-Arte, Kurt Redel, cond. Two 12-in. WESTMINSTER WAL 220.

——Radio Orchestra of Beromünster, Hermann Scherchen, cond. Three 12-in. LONDON LLA 2.

——Helmut Walcha, organ. Two 12-in. Archive ARC 3082/83.

——Josef and Grete Dichler, pianos. Two 12-in. WESTMINSTER XWN 2216.

——Gustav Leonhardt, harpsichord. Two 12-in. BACH GUILD BG 532/33.